365 Toddler Tips

A Helpful Handbook for the Early Years

365
Toddler
Tips

A Helpful Handbook for the Early Years

Penny Warner
with Paula Kelly, M.D.

Meadowbrook Press

Distributed by Simon & Schuster
New York

Library of Congress Cataloging-in-Publication Data

Warner, Penny.
  365 toddler tips : a helpful handbook for the early years / by Penny Warner.
    p. cm.
  Includes bibliographical references and index.
  ISBN 0-88166-464-2 (Meadowbrook Press) ISBN 0-684-02068-8 (Simon & Schuster)
  1. Toddlers. 2. Child rearing. 3. Toddlers—Development. I. Title

HQ774.5.W35 2003
649'.122--dc21

Editorial Director: Christine Zuchora-Walske
Medical Editor: Paula Kelly, M.D.
Editors: Nancy Campbell, Angela Wiechmann, Joseph Gredler
Production Manager: Paul Woods
Graphic Design Manager: Tamara Peterson
Illustrations: Lane Gregory
Cover Photos: RubberBall Productions, Getty Images, and Brand X Pictures
Index: Beverlee Day

Published by Meadowbrook Press, 5451 Smetana Drive, Minnetonka,
Minnesota 55343

www.meadowbrookpress.com

BOOK TRADE DISTRIBUTION by Simon and Schuster, a division of Simon and
Schuster, Inc., 1230 Avenue of the Americas, New York, New York 10020

09 08 07 06 05 04   10 9 8 7 6 5 4 3 2 1

Printed in the United States of America

Dedication

To Tom, Matthew,
and Rebecca—former toddlers.

Acknowledgments

Thanks so much to all who contributed
their expertise, especially Tracy Armstrong, Melanie
Ellington, Tiffany Gaddis, Anne Gilbertson, Claire
Johnson, Nancy Kindley, Holly Kralj, Isabel Lau, Dana
Mentick, Cindy Murphy, Ann Parker, Connie Pike, Chris
Saunders, Elby Salazar, Esther Skerritt, Vicki Stadelhofer,
Barbara Swec, Mary Warner, Sue Warner, Simonie
Webster, Susan Westerlund, and the Teabuds.
Thanks also to my wonderful editors, Dr. Paula Kelly,
Nancy Campbell, Angela Wiechmann, and Joe Gredler;
and to my publisher, Bruce Lansky.

Contents

Foreword

It happened so fast—that adorable baby you enjoyed cradling in your arms suddenly became a mobile toddler! However, no need to despair. Thanks to Penny Warner's *365 Toddler Tips*, you can pursue parenting your "ambulating wonder" with plenty of help and guidance.

Penny continues the same handy format of helpful hints you may have first encountered in the popular *365 Baby Care Tips*. The chapters are based on a toddler's ADL or Activities of Daily Living. They include some of the same topics found in *365 Baby Care Tips*, such as eating, bathing, and sleeping, but they also expand into toddler-specific areas. Tooth brushing, talking, nightmares, and, of course, that ever-important topic of toilet training are but a few of the issues covered.

Since many parents add a new family member during their child's toddler years, a section is included on preparing your child to be a sibling. And since statistics confirm that a toddler's chances of getting in harm's way escalate with his newfound mobility (and his appetite for adventure!), a huge and proper emphasis is paid to safety. Health care is appropriately highlighted, and the challenging area of discipline gets tackled as well.

Throughout, you'll find anecdotes of wisdom from other parents who have witnessed their toddlers' growth and development and who have some advice well worth disseminating.

As the parent of a toddler, you have so much to delight in as well as feel challenged by. I'm so glad *365 Toddler Tips* is available to help you in this new phase. Enjoy!

Paula Kelly, M.D.

Introduction

The toddler years, from age one to three, are some of the most exciting years in your child's life. As your child moves from babyhood to toddlerhood, she explores her independence and autonomy. She enhances her skills in all areas, making leaps and bounds in language, motor, cognitive, social, and psychological development. At the same time she tests the limits of her abilities and environment, which sometimes causes frustration for both of you.

365 Toddler Tips guides you through these exciting and challenging years. It offers you all kinds of ways to enjoy your child while you keep her safe and healthy and while you enhance her intellect, skills, and self-esteem.

The book is arranged by topics, including nutrition, hygiene, sleeping, health, toilet training, safety, discipline, playing, and many areas of development. The easy-to-read and convenient format puts thousands of ideas at your fingertips so you can quickly find answers to all your questions and concerns. In addition, you'll also find Quick Tips from experienced parents sharing their true-to-life stories and the lessons they've learned.

Toddlerhood is an adventure with many ups, downs, and in-betweens. Just turn the page and begin the adventure with your toddler.

Chapter 1
Nutrition and Mealtime

1. How Long Should You Breastfeed?

It's really up to you, but perhaps your toddler will influence your decision. Here are some points to help you decide whether to continue breastfeeding after the first year.

Doctor recommendation. The American Academy of Pediatrics recommends that women breastfeed their babies for at least 12 months. Child development experts have found that children who are breastfed for a year or more have higher IQs.

Nutritional needs. Your breastmilk's nutritional value changes after the first year, as do your baby's nutritional needs. If you continue to breastfeed past 12 months, know that your breastmilk cannot be the main source of nourishment for your baby.

Important questions. In the end, it's up to you to decide how long you want to breastfeed. How do you feel about breastfeeding? Are you still enjoying it? Has it become inconvenient? Does your toddler still seem interested? Examine your situation and try to make the best decision for both you and your child.

2. Weaning

When you're ready to wean your toddler from breastfeeding, here are some tips to ease the transition.

Talk to your child. Let him know you're thinking of not breastfeeding so often. Tell him he's growing up, becoming a big kid, and may soon stop nursing on his own. Express your pleasure at his independence.

Cut down slowly. Wean your child slowly by nursing less frequently and waiting longer periods of time between feedings. Give up one feeding at a time, and continue this for five or six days to allow your toddler—and your breasts—time to adjust. Save giving up the last night-time feeding until the end.

Create diversions. Keep your child distracted by engaging him in lots of activities so he'll be too busy to think about breastfeeding. If he needs a drink, give him a bottle of water or a cup of whole milk. Let him try out some of the many fun, easy-to-use cups and sippy cups.

3. Weaning from Bottle to Cup

It's exciting when your toddler begins to drink from a cup. He's reached another developmental milestone and is on his way to being more independent. Here are some ways to help him make the transition from a bottle to a cup.

Look for readiness. Most toddlers are ready to use a cup around 9 months, give or take a few weeks. If your toddler is able to grasp fairly well with his hand and fingers and can twist his wrist, he's probably ready for the cup.

Make it fun. Give your toddler a cup to play with so he becomes familiar with it before he really begins to use it. Let him use a cup in the bathtub to pour water or in the sandbox to pour sand. Once he's used to handling a cup, he'll be more ready to use it appropriately.

Buy a special cup. Take your toddler to the store and let him pick out the cup he wants. Or buy him a special cartoon cup you know he'll enjoy and give it to him as a gift. There are lots of choices, so think about the options, such as cups with one or two handles, cups with drinking spouts, cups with heavy bottoms, no-spill sippy cups, and so on. Make sure the cup is safe and nonbreakable, too.

Cup concerns. It's okay to let your toddler drink from a bottle now and then. Don't make an issue of it. Continue to try the cup, and talk about what a big kid he is now that he's using a cup. If your toddler is reluctant to use the cup, try a different liquid in it instead of his usual drink.

Spills are normal. Avoid overreacting to spills or you may make your toddler reluctant to use the cup for fear of spilling again. Just wipe up the spill and refill the cup. Fill it only halfway or less, so the spillage is minimal.

4. Quick Tip: Have a Tea Party

I let my toddler practice with his new cup by having a few tea parties. Using just a small amount of water, I let him practice filling and sipping and refilling the cup, over and over. We pretended the water was tea, milk, and juice, and we had fun enjoying each cupful. He made the change to a cup quickly after that—all because he thought using a cup was really fun.

—Tracy O.

5. Quick Tip: From Bottle to Cup

To help wean my toddler from a bottle to a cup, I started offering him a bottle with a straw instead of a nipple. He liked having the familiar bottle with the cartoon characters, but he thought it was fun to use a straw. Eventually he didn't need the straw anymore. Switching to a regular cup was the next logical step.

—Esther S.

6. Solid Foods

Near the end of the first year, solid foods gradually over-take breastmilk or formula as your baby's primary source of nutrition. Here are some tips for establishing solids as the main food source.

Fruits or veggies? Some parents begin with fruits because they're more appealing. Others choose vegetables, fearing that if fruits come first, their toddler might reject the veggies. Either choice is fine.

Grind your own. If your child prefers mashed foods, consider grinding up your own instead of buying commercial baby food. Use an inexpensive baby-food grinder. Many softer foods can simply be mashed with a fork.

One at a time. Introduce new foods one at a time so your toddler can get used to the taste and so you can make sure he isn't allergic to the food. If you notice itchy skin, a rash, hives, red cheeks, thick mucus from the nose or mouth, stomachache, or peculiar changes in behavior, stop offering the suspected food and call your doctor. Wait three to five days between each new food.

7. Nutritional Guidelines

Your toddler needs nutrients from each of the basic food groups, but don't worry if he doesn't get all of them in one meal or even in one day. As long as he eats something from each group over several days, he will have a balanced diet and will continue to grow. The basic food groups and number of daily servings follow.

- **Carbohydrates** (cereal, grains, rice, breads, pasta, potato)—6 or more servings
- **Fruits**—3 or more servings
- **Vegetables**—3 or more servings
- **Protein** (meat, poultry, fish, eggs, legumes)—2 servings
- **Dairy** (milk, cheese, yogurt)—2 servings
- **Fat** (oil, butter, margarine, mayonnaise)—use sparingly

8. Serving Suggestions

Here are some acceptable toddler-size serving suggestions for each of the food groups.

Carbohydrates
- ½–¾ cup iron-fortified cereal
- ½–2 slices bread or toast
- 1 small bagel or English muffin
- ¼–½ cup rice, potato, or pasta
- 10 French fries

Fruits and Vegetables
- ½ cup fruit
- ½–¾ cup fruit juice
  (100-percent juice, calcium fortified)
- ¼–½ cup vegetables

Protein
- 2–3 ounces tofu
- ¼ cup soft-cooked, mashed lentils, chickpeas, or beans (soy, pinto, kidney, navy, or other)
- 1 ounce skinless lean meat, fish, white-meat poultry
- 1 cooked egg (not more than 3 per week)
- 1 tablespoon peanut butter
- ⅓ cup tuna salad or chicken salad
- 1½ ounces lean meat
- 2½ ounces skinless dark-meat poultry
- 3 ounces salmon or other fatty fish
- ¾ kid-size burger
- 2 chicken nuggets

Dairy
- 1 cup whole milk (one-year-old)
- ¾ cup whole milk or 1½ cups 2% milk (two- and three-year-old)
- ¼–½ cup yogurt or cottage cheese
- ½ cup ice cream

Fat
- ½ tablespoon polyunsaturated oil, olive oil, canola oil
- ½ tablespoon butter, margarine, or mayonnaise
- 1–2 teaspoons salad dressing

9. Fun Finger Foods

Provide finger foods at snack time and mealtime so your child can feed himself. Make sure the foods are cut into small, safe pieces to prevent choking. (See Tips 133 and 134.) For the very young toddler, small ¼-inch cubes are about right. Here are some ideas for finger foods.

- Small pieces of bagels
- Ripe banana bites
- Dry, unsweetened cereal pieces
- Short strips or cubes of cheese
- Small crackers without sharp corners
- Soft fruits, such as pears or peaches
- Lunchmeats, especially chicken or turkey
- Pasta
- Rice cakes
- Sandwiches cut into fourths
- Soft-cooked veggies

10. More Fun with Finger Foods

Toddlers prefer bite-size snacks and treats because they're easy and fun to eat. Here are some ways to add even more fun to finger foods.

Cut them up. Cut larger foods such as eggplant, chicken, baked potato, and broccoli into smaller pieces so they're more manageable for your toddler.

Make a puzzle. Cut a piece of toast into simple puzzle pieces for your toddler to put together.

Dip it. Offer your toddler a variety of dips or sauces to enjoy with his finger foods, such as yogurt for fruit pieces, ranch dip for veggie bites, and ketchup for potato pieces.

Be creative. Instead of serving a regular peanut butter and jelly sandwich, cut it into an interesting shape such as a star or a simple design such as a boat, tree, or house. Cut fruits and vegetables into fun shapes, too.

11. Quick Tip: A-Dippin' and A-Snackin'

I found that a great snack is soft pretzels. I make them with the kids, tint them a different color each time, and use the dough to create interesting shapes. After the pretzels are baked and cooled, I give the kids some dipping sauces—such as melted cheese, honey, sweet-and-sour sauce, mustard, and ketchup—and let them dip and snack away.

—Brian Y.

12. Eating Habits Change

As your baby becomes a toddler, his eating habits and weight-gain rate change. His birth weight tripled by the end of the first year, but during the second year he'll gain only four to six pounds. This is normal.

Smaller appetite. As your toddler grows, his appetite shrinks. His tummy is still small, and he may not always be very hungry. Offer him small portions of food for that small tummy. Respect his natural inclinations about when he's full and when he wants more.

Snacks. Because your toddler's small tummy can't handle a lot of food at any one meal and because he burns food quickly, it's important to offer food more frequently. Healthy midmorning and midafternoon snacks are needed. Midway between meals, set out one or two foods such as raisins, apple slices, whole-wheat crackers, cheese cubes, or toast with peanut butter.

Too busy. Most toddlers experience an increase in energy as they learn to walk. Consequently, they're too busy exploring their world to take time for meals. About ten minutes and five minutes before a meal, let your toddler know it's almost mealtime to help him make the transition from playing to eating.

Quality over quantity. When your toddler does eat, try to make sure he gets nutritious foods (see Tip 7) over foods with empty calories and high-sugar snacks or desserts. He's more likely to eat healthy foods if he hasn't filled up on cookies and chips.

Preferences change. Be prepared. Toddlers' likes and dislikes change rapidly. The peas-and-carrot combination he gobbled up last week may be refused when offered again. Try rejected foods again from time to time—he may do another flip-flop. (See Tips 32–41.)

13. Quick Tip: Snack Time

My toddler used to ask for food all day long, which made me crazy. So I decided to pick two snack times during the day—ten o'clock and three o'clock. Snacks at these times took the edge off his hunger without ruining his appetite for lunch or dinner.

—Dana M.

14. Quick Tip: Limit Sugary Juices

My pediatrician told me to reduce the amount of juice I was giving my toddler because she was concerned about cavities and the possibility that my son wasn't getting enough nutritious foods. She suggested that I give him water in squirt bottles instead. As it turned out, my son loved to squirt the water into his mouth and hold his own bottle, and I didn't worry about tooth decay and loss of appetite.
—Rosa R.

15. Food Allergies

Some children have allergic reactions to certain foods. Possible symptoms include rash, hives, eczema, sneezing, runny nose, and wheezing. Some of the foods that commonly cause allergic reactions are cow's milk, egg whites, wheat products, oranges, and lemons. Other foods—peanuts, sesame seeds, shellfish, and other fish—may trigger more serious allergic reactions, including severe breathing problems that become life threatening. Such reactions require immediate medical assistance. Fortunately, young children are less often allergic to these potentially dangerous foods.

Watch for patterns. After your child has eaten a particular food, watch for a reaction that can occur a few minutes to a few hours after ingestion. Check with your doctor about the possible significance of any allergic reaction. If the reaction is repeated, stop offering the food.

Keep medication handy. If your child has a mild reaction, check with your doctor, who may suggest you give him an over-the-counter anti-allergy medication such as Benadryl. If your toddler has a strong reaction or if severe allergies run in your family, you may want to discuss allergies in more detail with your doctor. The less common but potentially life-threatening reactions may require using a device that automatically injects a premeasured dose of epinephrine, also called adrenaline.

See your doctor. Consider making an appointment with your doctor to have your child tested for possible allergies.

Medic alert tag. Make sure relatives, teachers, friends, and parents of friends are informed about your child's allergies and how to treat them. You may want to have him wear a medic alert tag if he has a severe allergy.

Be patient. Many children outgrow allergies over time. Most children outgrow egg and milk allergies by age four.

16. Quick Tip: Peanut Butter

The first time my son had an allergic reaction to peanut butter, I thought it was just a heat rash. But each serving of peanut butter produced a worse reaction. I didn't realize at the time that a skin rash is often a sign of an allergic reaction to food. When I finally figured it out, I stopped giving him peanut butter and talked to my doctor.

—Isabel L.

17. Quick Tip: Party Plan

Sometimes parents forget to tell other people about their kids' allergies. Whenever I host a birthday party, I always ask parents about their children's allergies so I know what to serve and what could be dangerous.

—Anne G.

18. Quick Tip: Irritable Bowel

I could tell my son was having cramps from his violent cries and the way he raised up his legs. I kept switching formulas, thinking he might be allergic to one of them, but nothing worked. I finally took him to a pediatric gastroenterologist, who said he was probably allergic to formula in general. This caused irritable bowel, which caused him to involuntarily withhold his bowel movements because he associated BMs with pain. We switched him from formula to soymilk and used a stool softener until he stopped the association.

—Claire J.

19. Sitting Pretty: Highchair Tips

Selecting the right highchair is the first step in mealtime setup and safety.

Sturdy design. Buy a highchair with a wide base and large tray so it's sturdy and well balanced.

Safe location. Keep the highchair away from dangers like the stove, kitchen counters, doorways, and high-traffic areas.

Sitting position. Don't allow your toddler to stand up in the highchair.

Buckled in. Always use the safety strap when your toddler is in the highchair, and make sure the tray is securely attached.

Gripper plates. Consider using plastic plates with rubber suction cups so your toddler won't be able to flip his plate off the tray.

20. Quick Tip: Keeping It Clean

A flannel-back vinyl drop cloth from a fabric store is perfect under a highchair. It's inexpensive, sold in wide widths, and cleans with a sponge. Throw it into the washing machine once a week on the gentle cycle, and dry on low heat.

—Isabel L.

21. Mealtime Philosophy

Your job is to make healthy, nutritious foods available to your toddler at regular intervals and to let your toddler be in charge of the kinds and amounts of foods he eats.

Keep it peaceful. Mealtime should be a happy experience, a time for the family to gather together, chat, play simple games, and enjoy food. Don't bring up problems, don't nag, and don't get into power struggles with your toddler over food.

Don't force your child to "clean his plate." Your parents may have insisted you eat everything on your plate—perhaps to avoid waste. Forcing your child to clean his plate, however, can lead to many power struggles and health problems like overeating and obesity. Keep portions small, let him eat what he wants from the foods on his plate, and let him stop when he feels the urge to stop.

Allow self-feeding. Let your toddler develop his fine motor skills, independence, and sense of competence by feeding himself. His awkward attempts will be messy at first, but with practice he'll soon become more coordinated.

Don't push seconds. Some parents equate feeding with love, and more feeding means more love. Acting on this mistaken belief can lead to overeating and obesity. Your toddler will ask for more if he wants it.

22. Mealtime Manners

Here are some tips for allowing your toddler to enjoy his food without making mealtime unpleasant.

Use plastic covers. Your toddler is going to make a mess no matter what. That's his job description. To minimize cleanup, cover the floor with plastic and cover your toddler with a large plastic bib.

Encourage utensils. After your toddler is adept with finger foods, give him easy-to-hold short utensils so he can learn to use a spoon and fork. Encourage him to try the utensils—even if he doesn't use them—and praise him when he does. (See Tip 23.)

No throwing or spitting food. There's nothing wrong with playing with food, but throwing or spitting food is unacceptable. If your toddler starts either of these behaviors, tell him firmly to stop—food belongs on his plate or in his mouth. If he continues to throw or spit food, tell him you're going to remove him from the table if he continues. Follow through if he does. If he agrees to stop, let him back up and praise him.

Avoid arguing about eating. Avoid turning mealtime into a battle. Keep the atmosphere pleasant by chatting, playing games, and so on. If your toddler doesn't want to eat, don't force it. Wrap up his food, put it in the refrigerator, and tell him it'll be there when he's ready to eat.

23. Learning to Use Utensils

As your toddler's fine motor skills (see Chapter 11) develop, he'll gain more control over his hands and fingers. Since one fine motor goal is self-feeding, here are some tips to help him learn to use utensils.

Fingers first. When your toddler begins to show interest in feeding himself, go ahead and let him do it. The sooner he starts, the sooner he will master the skills. Allow him to use his fingers, since he's still trying to master his fine motor control. Soon he'll progress to utensils.

Kid size. If you think your toddler is ready to try utensils, buy him a kid-size set that fits his hand. There are a variety of styles designed to help toddlers hold onto the utensils more securely and easily. Don't be tempted to let him try adult-size utensils because his probable frustration may keep him from practicing this skill. If you give him made-to-fit utensils right off the bat, he'll have success sooner and be less upset.

Ignore the mess. There's bound to be a mess when your toddler first tries utensils. Relax and let him experiment with these strange new tools. He just needs time to get acquainted with them. He'll soon get the hang of it, so try not to worry about the mess along the way.

Be flexible. Your toddler may not use the utensils the correct way all the time. That's okay. Just model the behavior—show him how you use yours—and let him do it his way until he's more comfortable coordinating the food and utensils.

Choose the right foods. Using utensils is tricky for little hands, so offer your toddler foods that are easy to scoop up with a spoon, such as mashed potatoes, macaroni and cheese, and puréed vegetables. Avoid foods like peas and spaghetti that are hard to manage, and foods that are too soupy.

24. Quick Tip: Hand to Mouth

When my toddler first started using a spoon, she would pick up the food with her hand, place it carefully in the spoon, then lift the spoon to her mouth. She knew she was supposed to use the spoon, but couldn't quite figure out how to manage it all. I thought she was pretty creative, solving her problem that way, so I just let her be. Eventually she learned how to spoon up the food correctly.

—Rocio S.

25. Make Mealtime Fun

The more appealing you make a food, the more likely your young toddler will eat it.

Make faces. With a little creativity you can turn a plain old sandwich into a clown face, monster face, and so on. Use bits of cut-up fruits and veggies to make eyes, a nose, a mouth, and so on.

Try silly shapes. Cut sandwiches, cheese slices, meat slices, and other foods with a fun-shaped cookie cutter. Or use a knife to create a spaceship sandwich, a house of cheese, meat on wheels, and so on.

Use fun dishes. Serve your toddler's snacks and meals on brightly colored plastic plates decorated with cartoon or other characters. You might want to buy a few plate-decorating kits that allow your child to personalize his own dishes.

Dazzle the drinks. Encourage your toddler to drink from a cup by offering him a decorated, spill-resistant mug. After he's learned to handle the mug, add a regular straw or a crazy straw for added fun.

Name that food. Use funny names for your young toddler's foods so they'll be more fun. Milk can be "moo juice," eggs can be "fluffy clouds," spaghetti can be "oodles of noodles," cheese and crackers can be "bitty bites," and so on.

26. Quick Tip: Playful Plates

I bought one of those make-a-plate kits kids can color with special markers. I let my daughter mark it up, then I wrote her name on it. We called it her "special plate." She loved it. She'd try just about any food as long as it was on her special plate. She's older now, but I still have that plate. I plan to give it to her when she has her own toddler.

—Diane P.

27. Quick Tip: Monster Cookies

I made "monster cookies" for my kids using a pumpkin cookie recipe and decorating them with monster faces. Instead of using canned pumpkin all the time, I occasionally replaced it with puréed frozen mixed vegetables. The vegetables didn't have a strong flavor, and the spices made them taste great.

—Tracy A.

28. Food Games

Another way to make mealtime more pleasant is to play games with your toddler while you eat.

Same and Different. Let your toddler compare and contrast the foods on his plate. Have him find the ones that look the same and the ones that look different. For example, both strawberries and cherry Jell-O are red; peas are smooth and raisins are wrinkled; both mashed potatoes and applesauce are soft; both Cheerios and ring pasta are round; cocoa is hot and ice cream is cold.

What's Missing? After asking your toddler to close his eyes, steal a few bites of food from his plate. Hide them under a napkin and have him try to guess what's missing.

What Is It? Tell your toddler to close his eyes, open his mouth, and wait for you to pop a bite of food in his mouth. Have him try to guess what it is.

Count 'Em. If your toddler has learned to count, have him count the bites as he eats.

Take Turns. Spoon a bite into your toddler's mouth, then let him do the same to you.

29. Kids in the Kitchen

Your toddler not only learns new skills from helping you cook, he's also more likely to eat the meals when they're done. There's always something he can do.

- Wash foods and utensils in the sink.
- Pour from small containers into bigger ones.
- Spread with a plastic knife or rubber spatula.
- Stir with a big spoon in a big bowl.
- Dip measuring cups into ingredients.
- Help set the table for a meal.
- Help clear the table when the meal is over.

Here's what he learns while he helps:

- Math (counting, measuring)
- Language (vocabulary, conversation skills)
- Motor skills (washing, pouring, stirring, mixing)
- Thinking (following directions, predicting the outcome)
- Science (combining ingredients, watching reactions)
- Self-esteem (feeling a sense of accomplishment and competence)

30. Quick Tip: Fun Fillings

Let your child help you decide what to make for a meal, then let him help you make it. Pigs in a blanket were a favorite with my kids. They loved rolling the hot dogs in the refrigerator rolls, and they loved eating them because THEY made them. They also enjoyed making tacos with different fillings, because they got to decide what to put in the shells. When they weren't making their own meals or snacks, they were often playing with their kitchen set and making meals with their toy foods.

—Cindy M.

31. Quick Tip: Cook Up Some Fun

I let my kids start learning to cook as early as possible. They loved creating their own snacks and helping with the meals. And they learned all kinds of skills—math, measuring, science, cooperation, patience. They were more likely to eat the food, too, when they helped make it.

—Orlando T.

32. Encourage a Picky Eater

Some toddlers (and some adults!) don't like one food to touch another on their plate. Some refuse food with certain textures or smells. Others insist on eating most of one food before starting another. And then there are many toddlers who just don't want to try new foods. If your child is a fussy or picky eater, don't give up hope. Here are some tips for helping him expand his experiences with food.

Don't give up. If your picky eater rejects a food the first time he sees it, back off for a while and reintroduce the food a few days or weeks (or months) later. Children's tastes change, and sometimes toddlers need to see a food several times before they try it (and like it).

Avoid "it's good" or "it's yucky." Avoid asking your toddler if he likes a new food or not. Instead, simply talk about its flavor, temperature, color, amount, texture, and so on. For example, you might say that squash has teeny-tiny vitamins that will help him grow strong or that squash tastes like orange mashed potatoes. This is also a good time to play some of his favorite food games. (See Tip 28.)

Avoid sweets. Sweets, soda pop, and junk food will kill a healthy appetite. When your picky eater's appetite is low, new foods will be even less appealing.

33. Picky Eater: Tricks of the Trade

Here are some creative tips to get new foods into your toddler's tummy.

Use funny names. Your toddler may be more likely to try foods that have funny names. Call bananas rolled in oatmeal "monkey bites," and chocolate milk "monster milk." Encourage him to think up funny names for other foods. Then when you serve them, use his funny name.

Try the "eat-to-find-it" surprise plate. Buy an inexpensive clear plastic plate to entice your toddler to try a new food. Cut out a fun picture from a magazine and tape it faceup under the plate. As your toddler eats his food, he'll be able to see the surprise picture.

Play detective. Ask him to be a detective who has to snoop out a "mystery" food. Give him time to thoroughly look at it, smell it, touch and move it, listen to it, and taste it before he reports his findings to you.

Color it. Sparkle it. Use a little food coloring to tint rice, cottage cheese, cream soup, plain yogurt, milk, and even water to make them more fun to eat and drink. Add a few decorative sprinkles to make new or rejected foods more inviting.

Combine old and new. Offer your toddler a smaller portion of a new food along with his usual portions of old favorites. Arrange them so the new food doesn't look too imposing on his plate.

Offer "new" foods. For example, if your toddler likes peas but doesn't like carrots, mix them together and see if he'll give the "new veggie" a try.

Different presentation. There's often a reason why your toddler doesn't like a food. It may be the color, texture, smell, or taste. Try altering the food somehow. For example, if your toddler doesn't like carrots steamed, shred them and mix them into a gelatin salad.

Flavor enhancement. Improve a food's flavor with another food that's more appealing. For example, add melted cheese, jam, ketchup, salsa, yogurt, fruit, honey, or some other topping your child likes.

34. Quick Tip: Popular Pops

My one-year-old was a really picky eater. I tried all kinds of foods and tricks to get her to eat healthy food. Finally my doctor recommended making frozen pops. They're fun to eat, taste good, and can be a great source of nutrition. I filled paper cups with fruit juice, mashed frozen fruit, and yogurt. Then I inserted a plastic spoon in the middle and put them in the freezer. She loved them!

—Julie B.

35. Picky Eater: Food 101

Sometimes toddlers don't like a food because of their fear of the unknown. Teach your toddler about a food so it's less foreign to him.

Learn about the food. Find out where it comes from, how it's made, why it's good for him, and how it can be served. For example, if you want to introduce zucchini, show your toddler how it grows, where to find it in the produce section, and how to use it for making a simple side dish, soup, salad, and snack.

Read books about food. Inspire your toddler by reading books such as *The Very Hungry Caterpillar* by Eric Carle, *Bread and Jam for Frances* by Russell Hoban, *Stone Soup* by Marcia Brown, and other books with food themes.

36. Quick Tip: Short-Order Cook?

I notice that many families have two different dinners—one for adults and one for children. I think this is a bad idea because, if done routinely, it delays the introduction of many new foods. I liked to mix "adult" foods with my kids' familiar meals so they were encouraged to try new things.

—Anne G.

37. Picky Eater: When All Else Fails

By age three, many toddlers are finished with the picky-eating phase and are more likely to try new foods. But if your toddler is still picky, here are some tips to handle the situation.

Lighten up. Don't pressure your toddler into eating new foods or changing his eating style—doing so can easily bring on a power struggle.

Relax. Your toddler won't starve himself. Try not to become anxious about his eating habits. Your child will notice your anxiety and wonder what's the matter.

Don't push it. Never force your child to eat. It can't be done. Don't get angry either, or punish your toddler for not eating.

Find alternatives. If you've tried everything and your toddler still resists, find alternatives to meet your child's nutritional needs. For example, if he doesn't like milk, offer him cheese, yogurt, ice cream, and other dairy products.

38. Quick Tip: Picky, Picky, Picky

My daughter was the pickiest eater of all time. For the first ten years of her life there were only ten foods she would eat—and not all at the same time. Her main problem was that she HATED the texture of most foods. If a food wasn't smooth, chances are she wouldn't eat it. Peanut butter and milk were her chief sources of protein. Finally, she began to eat more foods. So remember: Your picky eater will probably loosen up—eventually!

—Claire J.

39. Quick Tip: She Won't Starve!

I survived the picky-eater stage by telling myself my child wouldn't starve. I looked at what she was eating over the course of a week and noticed she was getting everything she needed. My pediatrician said that as long as she was growing and staying healthy, she was fine. I just kept introducing new foods, and eventually she ate them.

—Isabel L.

40. Quick Tip: Try and Try Again

If you want your toddler to try a new food, you may have to introduce it a gazillion times. She probably won't like it the first couple thousand times, but eventually she'll try it and—surprisingly—like it.

—Dana M.

41. Quick Tip: Don't Punish

I remember being sent to my room as a child when I didn't clean my plate. It never made sense to me because my mom was the one who filled my plate. She'd fill it too full with foods I didn't like. I had no say in the matter, yet I was punished when I didn't eat it all. I vowed I'd never do that to my child.

—Orlando T.

42. Going to Restaurants

Taking a toddler out for a meal can be a harrowing experience. Many restaurants aren't geared for young children, so you'll need to be prepared.

Call ahead. Ask the restaurant staff if they welcome children or if they have anything to offer toddlers, like kid menus, booster chairs, crayons, crackers, and so on. If they don't seem too accommodating, keep shopping.

Go to kid-friendly restaurants. Take your toddler to family restaurants that cater to children. They're more prepared to deal with the energy of young kids and will tend to overlook the noise and disruption. Plus, you'll be more comfortable if you don't have to worry about your toddler's behavior.

Ask for booth seating. If your child doesn't need a highchair anymore, ask the waiter for a booth so your child can spread out and enjoy his activities. Use a booster chair for added convenience.

Ask for crackers. If your toddler is especially hungry and you have no food with you, ask the host or server for some crackers, milk, or juice before ordering.

Bring activities. Always keep a supply of entertaining activities in your car, such as puzzles, coloring books, small toys, small books, and washable markers and paper. Grab a few of them on your way into the restaurant.

Play restaurant at home. When you're serving dinner to your toddler at home, make-believe you're at a restaurant and practice your restaurant behavior. Make a game of it and have fun.

Go at off times. Avoid going to a restaurant when it's busy or when your child is overly tired or extremely hungry. Long waits and a crabby child don't make for a happy mealtime.

Stay calm and positive. Be a good role model for your child at the restaurant. Be personable with the greeter and the wait staff. You might want to comment positively to your toddler about the nice table, window view, plants, and so on. Try being creative in describing the menu items he might like—for example, use a few silly voices. While waiting for your order, play quiet games with him, give him a small toy, and chat with him to help prevent potential misbehavior.

43. Quick Tip: Quick Service

Pick restaurants where you know the service is fast. It's unreasonable to expect young children to wait forty-five minutes or longer for their meals. No one will have a good time if the kids are hungry and bored.

—Claire J.

Chapter 2
Personal Hygiene

44. Time to Come Clean

When playtime is over, it's time to come clean. Here are some tips for washing your toddler from head to toe.

A daily bath? If your toddler doesn't like bath time, don't feel you need to bathe her every day. Too many baths can cause dry skin. Every other day or even twice a week is fine, unless your toddler gets extra dirty in between the scheduled bath days.

Make it quick. After your toddler is finished playing in the bath, wash her quickly. Don't draw it out.

Top to bottom. Wash your toddler from her face down. Use mild, fragrance-free, nonallergenic soap made for children, but go easy on it. A washcloth and warm water clean fine, except for especially dirty areas and genitals.

Shampoo last. Use a mild shampoo made for kids. Keep it out of your toddler's eyes, or let your child wear a visor to keep the suds out. Use conditioner if you need help with tangles after bath time. If possible, use a combination shampoo/conditioner to make the process faster and easier.

Towel dry. Wrap your toddler in a large towel after the bath and gently pat her dry–no rubbing!

Lotion? Powder? Especially if you bathe your toddler daily, you might want to use a fragrance-free, nonallergenic lotion to help with dry skin. If your toddler enjoys being powdered, use one made for kids.

45. Toys in the Tub

Bath time is a great sensory-motor experience. It offers your toddler a variety of sensations and properties to explore. Here are some ideas for toys and activities in the tub.

- Animal or other puppet washcloths for dramatic play
- Balls in a variety of sizes
- Bathtub activity centers
- Bubbles and bubble blowers
- Colorful soaps for washing and decorating skin
- Foam toys for soaking up water and squeezing
- Plastic and wooden boats
- Plastic cups and bowls
- Plastic dolls to soap and rinse
- Plastic spoons and other safe plastic kitchen items
- Rubber ducks and other plastic squeeze toys
- Small plastic pitchers, watering cans, or sprinkling cans for pouring
- Sponges in different shapes, colors, and sizes
- Squirt bottles for squirting and spraying
- Strainers and sifters
- Unbreakable, waterproof mirrors
- Washcloths for soaking, squeezing, and washing
- Waterproof bath books
- Waterproof, nonpermanent crayons for drawing on tub and tile

46. *Quick Tip: Tub Toys*

My son loves to play with squirt guns and squirt bottles in the water. I put dots of shaving cream on the sides of the tub, and he squirts them down. But we have a rule about keeping the water in the tub. If he deliberately squirts or pours water out of the tub, then it's time to get out!

—Susan W.

47. *Quick Tip: Keep It Short*

It was always a battle washing my daughter's hair. It was long and full of tangles, and she fought it every step of the way. I finally got her hair cut short—and what a difference! The whole process was a breeze. And she looked really cute with short, tangle-free hair.

—Shanice A.

48. Bath Time Is Play Time

If your toddler gets tired of all those toys in the tub, here are some fun ways to play with her in the water.

Sing songs. Voices always sound better in the bathroom. You can even record your songs and play them after bath time.

Make water noises. Put a straw in the water and blow bubbles. Slap the water with your hands. Capture air bubbles and let them go. Make noises underwater.

Massage your toddler. Use the water or soap as a lubricant, and massage your toddler's arms, legs, body, and head.

Make it rain. Sprinkle water lightly over your toddler's head or gently spray her with a mister so she can get used to having water on her face. Learning to cope with a little water on her face will help when she starts putting her head underwater when learning to swim.

Create a waterfall. Use a plastic cup or other container to pour water over your toddler's arms, legs, and body, and let her enjoy the sensation.

Sticker it. Put removable plastic stickers on the side of the tub for your toddler to play with.

49. Quick Tip: Washcloth Puppet

I made a puppet for my toddler out of two pastel washcloths. First I drew a puppet head, neck, and two hands on one washcloth, cut it out, and then cut out the other one to match. I sewed them together except at the bottom, and turned it inside out. I added details using permanent markers, and let my son give it a name. He loved to get washed with his bathtub puppet, and he had fun playing with it after he was washed.

—Holly K.

50. Quick Tip: Bath Stickers

My son loved to play with his homemade bath stickers. We cut out some fun characters and animals from old picture books and put them on the sticky side of clear Contact paper. Then we covered them with another sheet of Contact paper, and I cut out the pictures. During his bath, he dunked them underwater. Once they were wet, he could stick them onto the side of the bathtub and move them into different positions.

—Simonie W.

51. Quick Tip: Hair Salon

My toddler loved playing "hair salon." I left the shampoo in for a while so she could style her hair in crazy ways. Then I took pictures with our digital camera and showed her how her styles turned out. Eventually she started adding plastic flowers, fancy combs and clips, and costume jewelry.

—Dina W.

52. Songs in the Tub

Most toddlers enjoy their baths if they're given a chance to sing songs. Here are some tips for musical fun in the tub.

"Row, Row, Row Your Boat." Have your toddler sit on a washcloth and pretend it's a boat. Give her some plastic spoons and let her "row" as you sing the song.

"Ring around the Rosey." While you sing the song, hold your toddler in the water on her back and move her around in a circle. When it's time to "fall down," let go of her legs and hips (but not her upper body) so she has the sensation of falling.

"Twinkle, Twinkle, Little Star." While you sing the song, flick the water with your fingers to make "twinkling stars." When you get to "up above the world so high," raise your wet hands up and shake them over her head.

"Hokey Pokey." While you sing the song, have your toddler move each body part in and out of the water.

"Pop Goes the Weasel." While you sing the song, swirl your toddler in the water, then lift her up when you say "pop."

"Old MacDonald." While you sing the song, have your toddler make the animal noises and act out each animal in the tub.

53. Beyond Rubber Duckies

As your toddler grows and her cognitive skills increase, she's going to enjoy her time in the bath even more. She'll turn the bathtub into a water wonderland.

Teatime. Place a plastic tea set on a TV tray and let your toddler host an imaginary tea party for her floating friends. She can fill the teapot, pour tea, and float and sink the dishes. Add toy food snacks for even more fun.

Boat float. Supply Captain Toddler with a flotilla of plastic or wooden boats, and let her run races, sink battleships, and discover sunken pirate boats loaded with treasure.

Bath paints. Provide your toddler with bath paints so she can turn herself into a clown, monster, or superhero. Let her look in a mirror to see her creations.

Hoops and balls. Provide your toddler with small plastic hoops and balls so she can practice her shooting skills. Make your own hoops by cutting out the centers of plastic lids.

Silly squirters. Load the tub with all kinds of squirters: a squirt gun, squirt bottle, baster, and so on. Attach a sticker target to the tub wall, and let your toddler practice her squirting skills. Let her know there's to be no intentional squirting outside the tub.

54. I Don't Want a Bath!

If your toddler isn't in the mood for a bath—but she still needs one—here are some tips for getting her in the tub.

Offer choices. Avoid asking your toddler if she wants to take a bath. Instead, say, "Do you want to take your bath before the Barney show or after the Barney show?" That way she has some control over the situation.

Use kitchen items. Assemble some different items (waterproof and safe) from the kitchen for your toddler to play with in her bath. For example, you might include a wooden spoon, a baster, a whisk, measuring cups, small bowls, and plastic utensils. Then let her choose a few for tub time. She may want to play with items from her toy kitchen, too.

Rotate toys. Buy several bath toys and keep some in a cupboard in the bathroom. Rotate the toys each time so your toddler has something new to look forward to at bath time.

Do a penny hunt. Gather three pennies, and have your toddler sit in the bath and close her eyes. Then tell her to be very still and quiet and to open her ears. Toss a penny into the water and have your toddler listen for the sound. Then tell her to open her eyes and find the penny. When bath time is over, let her put the pennies in her piggy bank.

55. Dental Hygiene

It's important to establish good dental hygiene while your child is young. The condition of her baby teeth will affect her permanent teeth. Here are some things to consider regarding your child's dental hygiene.

Daily habit. Brushing now and then is not enough. Help her brush her teeth daily as part of her regular routine. While brushing twice a day is recommended, the most important time to brush is at bedtime. Leaving a coating of sugar on her teeth at night can lead to serious dental problems.

Fluoride. Check to see if your water is fluoridated. If it isn't, ask your dentist for fluoride drops.

Dentist. Talk to your dentist about having your toddler come in for a getting-acquainted visit. Most dentists want young children to get comfortable with the environment before the first checkup is performed. It's important for your child to form a positive attitude toward the experience.

Home checkups. After your toddler has brushed her teeth, make sure to praise her efforts. Then go over them yourself to ensure they're clean.

56. Tooth Brushing 101

It's important to teach your toddler good tooth brushing habits from day one. Here are some tips to keep in mind.

Toddler toothbrush. Let your toddler select a soft, kid-size toothbrush in her favorite color or style. There are lots of different types available.

Tasty toothpaste. Buy toothpaste in fun colors and flavors. Test a few flavors until you find one she likes. Remind her not to eat the toothpaste—it's not food—and put only a small dot on the toothbrush. She doesn't need much.

Teeth talk. Talk to your toddler about the importance of keeping her teeth clean, and explain what happens (tooth decay, pain) if she's not careful with brushing.

Doll practice. Give your toddler a doll with teeth, and let her practice brushing the doll's teeth with a small toothbrush. You can leave the toothbrush dry or add a little water if you like.

Copycat. Let your toddler watch you while you brush your teeth. Make funny faces in the mirror and funny sounds as you brush. Tell her how good your mouth feels afterward. Then let her give it a try.

57. Quick Tip: Got Teeth?

When my children began getting their teeth, I kept their teeth clean by wiping them off with a wet washcloth. I did this every night when I was washing their face or bathing them. I also had them watch me while I brushed my teeth. When it was time to help them brush their own teeth, they understood that keeping their teeth clean was important and brushing was a daily routine.

—Isabel L.

58. Quick Tip: Take Turns

First I let my son pick out his own toothbrush. Then I had him brush his teeth when I brushed mine. I let him watch how I did it, and then I let him take his turn. When he was done, I'd go over his teeth again. Then I gave him one last turn, which helped him feel like he was doing a good job. We had fun taking turns—Mommy's turn, then Seth's turn.

—Susan W.

59. Tooth Brushing Brush Up

As your three-year-old's fine motor skills increase, she's better able to take care of her teeth by herself. Some children, though, develop dental problems at this age that can affect their future permanent teeth. Here are three important reminders for promoting your older toddler's dental hygiene.

No skipping. It's often tempting to skip brushing on busy days or when your toddler's had a grumpy day. Be sure your toddler brushes all her teeth each day.

Touch up. Even after your toddler has developed good brushing habits, still continue to check and rebrush her teeth and gums to make sure they're really clean.

Trouble. If one of your toddler's teeth hurts or turns gray, or if she bumps a tooth or damages it in some way, call your dentist and have her check it.

60. Quick Tip: Brush to Music

When it's time for the kids to brush their teeth, I play a song they enjoy and tell them to brush until the song is over. It distracts them from the chore, and they can brush to the beat. Plus it keeps them brushing for at least two minutes.

—Jake B.

Chapter 3
Sleeping

61. Bedtime Basics

Your toddler's sleep habits will likely change during the next few years. He'll be busy and won't want to miss anything, and his growing imagination will sometimes keep him up at night. If you're having trouble getting your toddler to sleep, here are some ways to help.

Maintain a schedule. Try to wake up your toddler the same time each morning. Put him down for a nap at the same time each day and keep a consistent bedtime.

Release energy. Before you ask your toddler to settle down, make sure he's had an opportunity to release pent-up energy from the day. Do this an hour or more before bedtime, so he has plenty of time to calm down.

Wind down. Help your toddler calm down before a nap or bedtime so he'll be more inclined to go to sleep. Play a quiet word game, play soft music, watch a quiet video, read a story, take a bath, give him a massage, or talk about the day.

Avoid rambunctious activities. Don't tickle your toddler, roughhouse, or engage in rowdy play before bedtime. Also avoid sugary foods, scary TV shows, and scary stories.

Establish a ritual. Have your toddler go through a nightly ritual to get him in the proper frame of mind for sleep. For example, have him pick out a doll to sleep with, rock him, tell him a story, lie down with him, cover him with his blankey, and say a special goodnight.

Read a book about sleep. Read *Goodnight Moon* by Margaret Wise Brown, *Dr. Seuss's Sleep Book* by Dr. Seuss, *Time for Bed* by Mem Fox, or *The Going to Bed Book* by Sandra Boynton.

Do some relaxation techniques. Help your toddler relax his body from head to foot by having him focus on and relax each body part, one at a time. Talk to him about pleasant images such as a walk through a park, a basket of kittens, or a lake or river.

Help him feel safe. Use a night-light or soft lighting so the room isn't completely dark. If necessary, check on him every few minutes to let him know you're still there.

62. Quick Tip: Bedtime Rewards

We kept a chart of everything that needed to be done at bedtime: putting away toys, taking a bath, brushing teeth, getting into pajamas, and using the potty. Each time my kids finished one of their activities, they got to put a star on the chart. When the entire bedtime ritual was completed, they got to choose the bedtime book and the reader—Mom or Dad. At the end of the week, they got special rewards depending on how many stars they had. Both kids enjoyed doing this for several months.

—Cindy M.

63. The Family Bed

While many parents in other countries share their beds with their toddlers at night, the "family" bed remains a controversial issue in the United States. Here are some pros and cons.

The family bed may help kids:
- Feel more secure.
- Avoid sleep problems.
- Get to sleep faster.

On the other hand, the family bed may:
- Interrupt parents' sleep.
- Interfere with parents' intimacy.
- Reduce children's feelings of independence.

Some alternatives to the family bed include:
- Letting your toddler fall asleep in your bed, then moving him to his own bed.
- Moving your toddler's bed into your room.
- Lying down with your toddler in his bed until he falls asleep.

64. Quick Tip: Sleepover Night

Our daughter had always slept in her own bed, but one night she had a bad dream so we let her sleep with us. She loved to cuddle with us in our big, soft bed with the cozy comforter. After that night, we decided to make a special "sleepover" night once a week when she would sleep with us. We read lots of bedtime stories, talk about what fun things we have planned for the next day, and wish each other sweet dreams. With our busy lives, it's magical to spend a peaceful, quiet night cuddled together. Being physically close makes us feel emotionally close, too. For us, sharing a family bed every night is not the best option, but while she's still young, we all love our sleepover tradition.

—Shanice A.

65. Moving to a Big Bed

At some point your toddler will outgrow his crib and be ready for the "big-kid" bed. Here are some tips for choosing the right time and making a smooth transition.

Is your toddler ready? Talk to your toddler about moving to the big bed before it actually happens. If your toddler seems reluctant for any reason, delay the change to avoid unnecessary problems.

Take your time. Don't rush the change. Talk to your child about growing up and all the wonderful things he'll experience as a big kid.

Let your toddler help. When you both decide it's time to make the move, let your child help with the transition. If you need to buy a new bed, take him with you and let him help select it. Also let him help move furniture around to make space for the bed.

Buy fun sheets. Let your toddler help pick out the sheets, comforter, and other bedding. Kids often prefer cartoon characters and bright colors, so let him choose his favorites.

Don't forget the lovey. If your child is reluctant to move out of his crib because of all the special loveys (teddy bears, dolls, blankets, pacifiers) that "live" there, tell him they can move to the big bed, too. This is not time to wean him from his security toys.

Maintain rituals. Do the same things you did when putting your child in the crib. Read a story, use a night-light, get rid of the monsters, and so on.

Prepare for a new baby. If you're expecting a new baby, try to complete your toddler's transition to the big bed a few months before the baby arrives. Doing so will help prevent your toddler from associating the bed change with the displacement he's likely to feel when the baby comes. (See Tip 316.)

66. Quick Tip: His Own Bed

Our son was in bed with us until he was two. At that point we decided a change was necessary because we weren't sleeping well with him in there. First we talked to him about how much fun it would be for him to get his own bed. Then we went out and bought a new twin bed, a comforter, cartoon sheets, and a pillow—all of which he helped pick out. We decided to put him to bed a bit later than usual that first night so he'd be tired. We read him a book, kissed him goodnight, and told him we'd be right in the next room. We also told him he needed to stay in his own bed all night. We said if he did that, he could choose a special breakfast in the morning. Lo and behold, at 7:30 the next morning he crawled out of bed, proudly told us that he slept in his own bed all night, and asked for waffles for breakfast. We haven't had any problems since.

—Susan W.

67. Bedtime Stories

Some children have a hard time relaxing at bedtime after a stimulating day of action and adventure. Help your child get to sleep by creating "dreamscapes"—fantasies that help him unwind and take him off to dreamland. Speak slowly toward the end of the story and try to come up with a calming, soothing ending. Here are some suggestions.

Trip to Disneyland. Take your toddler on an imaginary trip to Disneyland or some other kid-friendly destination. Join Mickey and his friends for a make-believe walk through the park, and let your toddler "ride" on some of his favorite rides. If you can tell Disneyland is too exciting for going to sleep, move on to a beautiful lake, river, bird sanctuary, garden, rainbow, or other restful spot.

Fun with a friend. Create a story about your toddler and his best friend, and weave a dreamscape where wonderful things happen.

Character caper. Have your toddler choose one of his favorite characters, such as Barney, and take them on a journey around the neighborhood, city, or world to discover various wonders together.

Movie magic. If your toddler has a favorite movie, recreate the story by adding your child to the action and including him in the adventures. Make sure he's the hero, and avoid the scary parts before bedtime.

68. Quick Tip: Never-Ending Story

We had a bedtime tradition that got started by accident. One night I began telling my daughter a story, and she fell asleep before I finished it. The next night she wanted to know how the story turned out. I asked her what she remembered, and then I picked up the story from that point. The same thing happened that night; she fell asleep before the story ended. So we just kept continuing the story night after night. I don't think it ever ended.

—Stefan C.

69. Quick Tip: Sleepytime Fun

At bedtime, we made a habit of telling our son that something special would happen the next day, so he had something to look forward to when he woke up. Sometimes it was a special cereal, a fun play date, an outing to the zoo or library—things like that. We also said if he wasn't tired he could play in bed, but he couldn't get out of bed. He usually fell asleep while playing.

—Susan W.

70. Stalling at Bedtime

If your toddler puts up a fight at bedtime or if the nighttime ritual stretches out and seems endless, here are some more tips for getting him to bed and to sleep.

Five-minute lead time. When it's almost time to go to bed, set a timer and let your toddler know he has five minutes until bedtime. This way he knows bedtime is soon but not now, he has a chance to get used to the idea, and he can bring his play to a close. The timer relieves you of the role of "enforcer."

Last story. Choose a book that will be the "last story" of the night, or better yet have your child choose it. After you've read a couple of books, read the selected "last story." He'll know that it's time to go to sleep after the book is finished. If he's made the choice, he'll feel more in control of the situation and may be more cooperative.

One-drink limit. If your toddler has a habit of asking for a drink of water at bedtime, he's probably stalling. Anticipate this request by offering him a drink before he gets into bed. Tell him he has a one-drink limit. This is especially helpful if he's trying to stay dry at night. (See Tip 126.) After he's had his drink, that's it.

Monster mash. Rid the room of monsters (see Tip 73), if necessary, and then tell your toddler it's safe to go to sleep.

Loveys. Let your child choose a special lovey to keep him company at bedtime. He might choose the same one each night, select from an assortment of favorites, or he might want them all in bed every night—whatever helps him feel secure.

Positive reinforcement. Praise your toddler when he gets into bed on time, and let him know you're proud of him for sleeping in his own bed. Praise him the next morning, too.

71. Keeping Your Toddler in Bed

Some kids don't like to stay in bed once the light is turned out and you've said goodnight. If your toddler tends to get out of bed frequently, try some of the following tips to help him stay put.

Let him play. Keep a few quiet toys near your toddler's bed. Let him know he needs to stay in bed, but if he can't fall asleep, he can play quietly in bed. Pile some picture books and board books near his bed, and encourage him to look at them until he falls asleep.

Give him a flashlight. Let your toddler play with a flashlight in bed with the lights out.

Offer a reward. Tell your child that if he stays in bed all night, he can have a special reward in the morning. The reward might be sliced strawberries for breakfast, a simple art project, a walk outside to look for squirrels, or a phone call with Grandma. Don't give him something that's normally off-limits, however, such as candy for breakfast. Make sure to follow through with a reward each time he stays in bed all night. Discontinue the reward when you think he's ready.

Use a gate. If nothing else works, put up a gate as a last resort.

72. Getting Back to Sleep

Some toddlers have trouble sleeping through the night because of their excess energy. If your toddler wakes up and cannot get back to sleep, here are tips to help.

Cuddle. Hold you toddler and rock him back to sleep in your arms. He may need the extra security you provide by holding him.

Offer a snack. He may be hungry after using up so much energy during the day, or he may need something to settle his stomach. Keep it light, bland, and comforting, such as yogurt, Jell-O, or a cracker and a sip of water.

Massage. Stroke your toddler and give him a slow massage to relax his muscles and ease his tension. You might focus on one area of the body, such as his feet, legs, shoulders, neck, head, or forehead. Or massage him all over.

Tell a story. Tell your toddler a repetitive story in a soft voice to get his mind off any concerns and lull him back to sleep. Don't make the story too exciting, though. In fact, you might tell the same story each time he wakes up in the night.

Provide comfort. Give your toddler his pacifier, or surround him with stuffed animals to give him comfort. Make sure his special blanket is close by.

Reassure. Tell him you're right down the hall and can hear him if he needs anything. Tell him he's safe and you'll always be there to protect him.

73. Coping with Monsters and Nightmares

Your toddler's imagination may occasionally get carried away with the "dark side" of things. Even though you frequently tell him there are no monsters, he may continue to believe there are, or he may fear inanimate objects will come alive. Here are some ways to scare those monsters away until he realizes there aren't any.

Tell him the truth. Remind your toddler that there's no such thing as monsters. It may take time for him to believe it, but keep saying it.

Read a happy story. Put your child in a pleasant state of mind at bedtime so he can drift off to sleep without negative thoughts.

Use night-lights. Plug in a night-light so your child can see his room is clear of monsters. Try to arrange the furniture to keep large shadows to a minimum. Or let him shine a flashlight into all the nooks and crannies of his room before he goes to sleep.

Do a bed check. If your toddler still insists monsters are lurking about, do a thorough check of your toddler's bedroom while he watches. You might want to announce "All clear, no monsters here" while you search.

Offer protection. Use a water spritzer to spray away monsters wherever your toddler points. Or wave a magic wand over your toddler's room for protection. You can also put a "watchful" doll or teddy bear near your child's bed.

Talk about his dreams. If your child wakes up from a bad dream, sympathize with him and remind him that dreams aren't real. Talk about the dream to help him understand it and allay his fears.

Calm him after nightmares. If your child cries out from a nightmare, check on him immediately. Reassure him that everything is okay, and use a soothing voice to talk him back to sleep.

74. Quick Tip: Monster Check

Every night we would have Daddy check for monsters under the bed and in the closet to make sure the room was monster-free. This worked well for our son, who really believed in monsters. It was simple to do and it seemed to reassure him.

—Susan W.

75. Quick Tip: Monster Stories

When my kids thought there were monsters under the bed, I began reading them books on the subject. It worked well because they related to the story, and it helped them understand that there just weren't any monsters.

—Claire J.

76. Early Risers

Some toddlers are extremely early risers—sometimes way too early for Mom or Dad! Most of these toddlers outgrow this habit by their early elementary years. Until then, here are some tips that may help your child sleep a little later.

Encourage exercise. Encourage your child to exercise vigorously, and gradually increase the length of his exercise periods or their frequency. Spend more time outdoors in the fresh air. For balance, schedule some quiet, relaxed times from late afternoon to bedtime.

Avoid late afternoon naps. Not only do late afternoon naps often interfere with going to bed and getting to sleep, they may also lead to early morning wake-ups.

Limit fluids after dinnertime. Avoid excess fluids an hour and a half before bedtime. A soaked diaper may be causing your toddler to wake in the wee hours.

Extend his bedtime. Try moving his bedtime ten minutes later each night for about three to six days. If the bedtime was 7:00, it will now be 7:30 or 8:00. Caution: It's usually not useful to keep a toddler up extremely late, as overtired toddlers seldom sleep well or late.

Slow your response. Wait ten or fifteen minutes—even if your early-riser is crying—before you rush in to pick him up. He may cry for a while and then go back to sleep.

Block out light and noise. Some toddlers are woken by early morning light, so you might want to add an opaque, room-darkening shade to his window or switch to heavily lined curtains or drapes. If the jarring noise of garbage trucks or other clatter is a suspected culprit, try running a fan or humidifier on a low setting in his room. Its constant nearby drone may buffer the louder noises.

Let him play. If your toddler is an early riser, place some small toys in his crib or on his bed after he's asleep. He may decide to play with them when he wakes up, giving you another half hour of sleep.

Accept what you cannot change. If all else fails, you may have to accept that you yourself will need to go to bed an hour or two early so you won't become too exhausted from rising early with your child.

77. Quick Tip: Awake at Dawn

I had a real problem keeping my son in bed in the wee hours of the morning. He was an early riser and would wake everyone else up at the crack of dawn. We tried lots of things but the only trick that worked was keeping him up longer at night. That seemed to change his sleep clock, and we were able to get a little more sleep in the morning.

—Anne G.

78. Quick Tip: It's Too Early!

We put together a basket of toys that the kids could play with when they woke up early. The only rule was they had

to stay in bed to play with them. We told them their beds were "islands." They could take whatever they wanted from the basket to their island, but they couldn't get off the island until Mom or Dad said it was safe. They loved this game, and it usually gave us an extra half hour or so.

—Cindy M.

79. Quick Tip: Take Turns

Our kids woke up really early in the morning, which wasn't a problem during the week, but on the weekend we really wanted to sleep in. My husband and I finally found a solution. We took turns getting up with the kids. He'd take Saturday morning while I slept in, and I'd take Sunday morning and let him sleep in. The next weekend I'd take Saturday and he'd take Sunday. This allowed each of us to catch up on sleep at least one morning a week.

—Claire J.

80. Quick Tip: TV Snooze

We taught our son how to turn on the TV so he could watch cartoons on Saturday morning while we slept in. We turned the TV to the desired station the night before, and we adjusted the volume so it wouldn't be too loud. We reminded him to be quiet if he wanted to play. We also made a snack and put a sippy cup of milk in the fridge so they were ready for him when he woke up. He'd turn on the TV, get his milk and snack, and eat at the table while he watched his shows. He was proud of his independence, and we were grateful for the extra sleep.

—Susan W.

81. Quick Tip: Comic Relief

My husband started reading the Sunday comics to our son when he turned three. He picked appropriate comics he thought our son would enjoy. After reading the speech balloons and captions, they would play "find the differences" among the pictures. I loved it because I could stay in bed and get some extra sleep. My boys are now eight and fourteen, and they still look forward to this routine each Sunday morning.

—Isabel L.

82. Naptime: Getting Your Toddler to Sleep

Naptime is an important part of your toddler's daily routine. It gives him the chance to relax his body and recharge his batteries after using a lot of energy early in the day. But some toddlers don't want to take naps for fear of missing all the fun (or because they're in a negative period). If your child is having trouble taking a nap, here are some tips to help.

Relaxation time. Instead of calling it "naptime," which may be the source of the problem, tell your toddler it's "relaxation time" and lie down with him. Massage his forehead and tell him to relax each body part as you smooth away his tension. Move down to his cheeks, his neck and so on, all the way to his feet. Talk to him in a soothing voice as you go, and he should be asleep before you get to his toes. If not, at least he'll be relaxed for a while. (Start the relaxation at the same time each day so your toddler understands it's a routine.

Slow breathing. Lie down together and do some slow breathing. Whispering, count to three with each inhalation and exhalation. (Start counting at a normal rate, then gradually slow it down.) Have your toddler try to follow your breaths, which should relax him as his breathing slows. Be advised: This technique can cause you to drift off, too!

Soft music. Put on some soft music and have your child lie down, close his eyes, and listen. Tell him to picture a scene that fits the music, or tell him a story that matches the soothing music.

Rest period. If you toddler just won't sleep, it could be he's just not tired. Have him lie or sit in bed for a period of time to take a break. Allow him to play with a few of his toys or read a book in bed, then let him up when the time has elapsed. He may surprise you and fall asleep among his toys.

83. Quick Tip: Rockabye Toddler

When my toddler started giving up naps at age two, he got really cranky, but he just wouldn't lie down for a nap. Finally I just held him and rocked him in our old rocking chair. I sang him a song as I rocked, just like I used to when he was a baby. After a few minutes of rocking and singing, he'd begin to relax and then fall asleep. I think it was the warmth of my body, the gentle rocking, the soothing voice, and the comfort of my arms that helped him finally relax enough to nod off. And I enjoyed our snuggling time. I knew it wouldn't be long before it was over for good.
—Susan W.

Chapter 4
Physical Health

84. Keep Up with Vaccinations

Keeping your toddler healthy includes regular visits to the doctor, even when your child isn't sick. Immunizations are a part of those visits; they keep your toddler free from life-threatening diseases. Here's a basic immunization schedule for a toddler, as recommended by the American Academy of Pediatrics. Contact your doctor to determine your child's specific schedule.

- **HepB:** Your child should receive her third dose of the hepatitis B vaccine between 6–24 months.
- **Varicella:** Your child should receive the varicella (chickenpox) vaccine between 6–24 months. This is often done near your child's first birthday.
- **DtaP:** Your child should receive a fourth DTaP (diphtheria, tetanus toxoids, and acellular pertussis) vaccine between 15–18 months.
- **Hib:** Your child should receive her fourth Hib (Haemophilus Influenza type B) vaccine between 12–15 months.
- **MMR:** Your child should receive her MMR (measles, mumps, and rubella) vaccine between 12–15 months. This is often done near your child's first birthday.
- **PCV:** Your child should receive her pneumococcal conjugate vaccine between 12–15 months.
- **IPV:** Your child should get her third inactivated polio vaccine between 6–24 months. This is usually done around 18 months.

85. When to Call the Doctor

It's sometimes difficult to know when your toddler is really sick enough to call the doctor. Here are some symptoms that may require medical attention.

- Blood in urine or BM
- Breathing with difficulty
- Burns with blisters
- Change in appearance or color
- Change in behavior
- Constipation
- Convulsions
- Persistent cough
- Diarrhea with blood, mucus, fever, or foul smell
- Ear pain or rubbing side of head
- Discharge from ears
- Eyes red or filled with pus
- Fever (See Tip 88.)
- Ingestion of nonfood item
- Listlessness for over a day or two
- Loss of appetite or disruption in feeding pattern
- Vomiting with force or vomiting that's different from normal
- Sensing that something is definitely wrong with your child

86. Calling in an Emergency

If you need to call the clinic or your child's doctor in an emergency situation, be sure you can quickly relay the following information.

Temperature. Before you call, take your child's temperature. The doctor will not only need to know the reading but the type of thermometer you used. (See Tip 87.)

Medications. Know the name, strength, and dosage of any medication (both over-the-counter and prescription) your toddler is taking.

Weight. Know your toddler's weight in case the doctor needs it to prescribe a medication.

Condition. Be prepared to tell the doctor specific details about your toddler's condition—her color, behavior, energy level, skin reactions, and so on.

Allergies. Note any allergies or other medical problems your child has so the doctor can take those into account.

Estimate. If your toddler has ingested something she shouldn't have, try to estimate how much of the substance was consumed. Also estimate how long it's been in her system.

Antidote. Keep syrup of ipecac available to induce vomiting, but use it only if your doctor or another trained health care professional instructs you to do so.

87. Taking Your Child's Temperature

If you suspect your child has a fever, you should take her temperature before calling the doctor so you can give the doctor as much information as possible. Be sure to tell the doctor what type of thermometer you used.

Rectal thermometer. This is the most accurate thermometer for measuring your child's temperature. However, if you have a squirmy toddler or you're not comfortable using one, it may not be the best option.

Axillary (armpit) thermometer. This gives a fairly accurate reading that's one degree lower than a rectal reading. Hold it under your child's armpit, make sure she keeps her arm against her chest, and wait for the beep.

Tympanic (ear) thermometer. This is a fast and easy option and is similar to the one your doctor uses, but it's expensive. Place a disposable cover over the tip of the instrument, insert it gently into your child's ear, and wait for the beep.

Thermometer strip. This is also quick and easy, but it gives the least accurate reading. Place the strip on your child's forehead and read the results.

No mercury. Mercury thermometers are no longer recommended. If you drop a glass thermometer and it shatters, the mercury inside could pose a serious health risk to your child.

88. Fevers: What to Do

If you take your toddler's temperature and discover she has a fever, here's what to do.

- Over 105°F rectally (or equivalent)—call doctor immediately
- 104–105°F rectally (or equivalent)—call within 24 hours
- 102–104°F rectally (or equivalent)—call during regular office hours
- Under 102°F rectally (or equivalent)—if the low-grade fever lasts for more than three days, call during regular office hours

89. Quick Tip: Fever and Fluids

If your child has a fever and needs to take fluids, buy Popsicles or make them and keep plenty on hand. They're great for reducing fever, providing necessary fluids, and generally helping your child feel better.

—Claire J.

90. Quick Tip: High Fever Reaction

My daughter once had a horrible ear infection that caused her fever to climb to 104°F. I rushed her to the doctor's office, and they put her on antibiotics. The next day she complained that her feet hurt. I found they were covered in hives. I called the doctor's office again, thinking she was going into anaphylactic shock or something. The nurse told me that hives sometimes occur as an allergic reaction to a high fever.

—Claire J.

91. Teething Pain

Most toddlers have eight teeth by the time they reach their first birthday. These are usually incisors—the thin, sharp teeth in front that are used for biting. Incisors usually break the gums more easily than molars, which start to appear around 12–15 months and are usually in by 24 months. Molars are bigger and broader and are used for chewing. Because they have a harder time breaking through the gums, they usually cause more pain. Here are some tips for helping your toddler cope.

Check the gums. If you suspect your toddler is having teething pain, check to see if her gums are red and swollen. Use your finger to rub along the gum line to feel for firm bumps (emerging teeth) underneath.

Discourage sucking. When your toddler sucks on a bottle, pacifier, or thumb, the sucking action draws blood to the gum area, which increases the pain. Encourage her to use a cup, if possible.

Offer relief. Give your toddler something cold to chew on, such as a cold teething ring, a cold wet washcloth, a frozen bagel, or a frozen banana. Apply pain reliever directly to your toddler's gums, or give your child acetaminophen in age-appropriate doses.

See your doctor. Fever, loss of appetite, diarrhea, and vomiting are usually signs of illness—not teething pain—so call your doctor if they occur.

92. *Quick Tip: Cool Cure-All*

Popsicles are great for the pain of teething and for other mouth injuries, too.

—Dana M.

93. Colds and Cleanliness

Although three-year-olds are generally healthier and have fewer ear infections, stomachaches, and allergic reactions than younger toddlers, they seem to have more runny noses and common colds, which they pick up from contact with other kids. Here are some tips to help keep your older toddler healthy.

Friends are important. Even though kids pick up illnesses from other kids, don't limit your child's interaction with friends. The social skills she gains are more important than an occasional runny nose.

Household germs. Don't be overly worried about household germs. Your child has built up an immunity to most of them.

Clean toys. Wash your child's toys at least once a week to help kill germs. Wash them right away after they've been handled by a sick child or a lot of children.

94. Quick Tip: Pacifier Problem

My toddler was still using a pacifier at 20 months, which really didn't bother me. He seemed to need it and I didn't see any reason to take it away. But what did bother me was that he was always dropping it on the floor and getting it dirty. Finally I bought a dozen of them and told him to get a fresh one from the pacifier bowl every time he dropped one. When the bowl was empty, we collected the dirty ones, washed them all at once, and started over again.

—Lin L.

95. Home Remedies

If your toddler is sick, first determine if you need to call the doctor or nurse line. (See Tip 85.) If the situation doesn't warrant a visit to the clinic, here are some tried-and-true home remedies.

Stuffy nose and sore throat. Make some chicken soup or hot broth to help open your child's nasal passages and soothe her sore throat. Test the soup or broth first to make sure it won't burn your child's mouth.

Runny nose. Mix 1 teaspoon salt into 1 cup lukewarm water. Use a nose dropper to squeeze two to three drops into each nostril as needed, usually before meals and bedtime.

Chapped nose. Spread a little petroleum jelly around the nasal area to protect the skin from becoming overly chapped and bloody.

Earache. To reduce inflammation and swelling, fill a hot water bottle, cover it with a towel, and hold it against the sore ear. Numbing eardrops also help some children get relief until they can be seen in the doctor's office.

Diarrhea. Put your child on a BRAT diet (bananas, rice, applesauce, and toast) to help firm up her stools. As the diarrhea begins to disappear, give her yogurt to help get her intestinal bacteria back in balance.

Vomiting. Wait an hour or so after the last vomiting, and give your child a few sips of ginger ale or a sports drink like Gatorade (but not water) every ten minutes. Double the amount every hour if there's no problem. Wait eight hours before giving food, then start with small amounts of bland foods like crackers or toast. Resume a normal diet after twenty-four to forty-eight hours if the vomiting has ended.

Croup. If your toddler has a harsh barking cough, use a humidifier or vaporizer. Alternatively, let her breathe in some moist night air, or open your freezer door and let her breathe the cool air. Sitting in the bathroom with a hot shower running may also help.

Pinkeye. Soak cotton balls in warm water and place them on your toddler's closed eye to soothe the pain and itching.

Stye. Dip a bag of black tea in warm water, squeeze out the excess liquid, and place the bag on the closed eye for ten minutes.

96. *Quick Tip: Humidifier Woes*

Humidifiers are great when your toddler has a cough. But avoid using a humidifier in one location for weeks and weeks. You may ruin your ceiling—the way I did.

—Dana M.

97. *Quick Tip: Band-Aid Miracles*

My little boy was always falling down and getting scrapes and bruises. He was full of energy and hard to keep up with, and he wasn't afraid to push his limits. Instead of restricting him, I let him test his abilities—under close supervision, of course. When he fell or banged himself, he usually brushed it off. For the bumps and bruises that didn't go away so easily, I applied the magical cure of a cartoon Band-Aid. I was always amazed at its healing power.

—Dana M.

98. *Quick Tip: Boo-Boo Bunnies*

When my child gets a bump or bruise, I give her a Boo-Boo Bunny. You can buy them or make them out of washcloths fashioned into a bunny shape. There's a space in the middle that holds an ice cube to help reduce swelling and make your child feel better. It works almost as well as a parent's kiss—and is especially helpful for babysitters.

—Anne G.

99. Before the Doctor Visit

Some children begin to fear doctor visits at an early age. Being examined by a stranger in a strange place that smells funny makes some kids anxious and unhappy. Here are some tips to help ease your toddler's fears.

Prepare your child. Every few months, spend a few minutes talking to your child about why doctors are important and what happens at a doctor visit. Natural times for such a talk are when one of her siblings, other relatives, or friends needs to go to the doctor.

Read books about doctor visits. Read to your child some of the many children's books about going to the doctor. The storylines will answer many of her questions and concerns. They will also echo what you have already told her.

Play doctor at home. Give your toddler a toy doctor's kit and a doll so she can act out both her perceptions and her fears about going to a doctor. Such play will help her become more at ease and also help her feel more in control of the situation.

Be honest. Don't lie to your toddler about what's going to happen during an upcoming checkup, or she'll stop trusting you. You don't have to go into great detail, but be honest.

Bring a lovey. Ask your child to choose a favorite stuffed animal or blanket to bring along to the doctor's office to give her added comfort.

100. During the Doctor Visit

Now that you've prepared your toddler prior to your appointment, here are some tips to keep her at ease during the doctor visit.

Bring toys. In case there's a wait before you see the doctor, bring some toys or books for your toddler to enjoy. These may also provide a distraction while the doctor examines your child.

Offer a surprise. You may want to tell your toddler you have something special waiting for her when she's finished with her doctor visit.

Greet the doctor. Show the doctor you're happy to be there so your toddler sees you're not afraid. Try not to show mixed feelings.

Examine Dolly first. Ask the doctor if he or she would first give your toddler's doll a "checkup" so your child has an idea of what to expect.

Keep her company. Stay with your child the whole time you're at the doctor's office.

Praise her afterward. The best reward is to tell your toddler how proud you are of her and what a big kid she's becoming.

101. Quick Tip: Make It Special

Every time I take my son to the doctor, we make it a special outing by going for ice cream or lunch or by heading to the park or playground after we're finished. That way he has something to look forward to when we're done at the doctor's office. It's been very effective in reducing his anxiety about going to the doctor.

—Charles F.

102. Well-Child Visits

Most pediatricians recommend you begin annual well-child visits at age two. Here's what your doctor will check.

Health history. If your doctor isn't familiar with your toddler, he or she will want to know about your child's prenatal period, birth, and illness history and whether she's at risk for any health problems. Be sure to mention anything in partic- ular that concerns you.

Growth chart. Your toddler's height and weight will be measured and compared with a standard growth chart.

Daily habits. Your child's eating, sleeping, urinating, and bowel-moving patterns will be reviewed.

Development. The doctor will check your toddler's overall physical, emotional, behavioral, cognitive, and social development to see if there have been any problems.

Safety. The doctor will also want to discuss your child's environment and any safety issues that need to be addressed.

Physical exam. The doctor will examine your toddler's appearance, activity level, responsiveness, and interactions with her environment. He or she will listen to your toddler's heartbeat; check her eyes, ears, and throat; and look at her breathing, reflexes, and physical movements.

Immunizations. If your child has missed any immunizations, your doctor may have them done at the well-child visit. (See Tip 84.)

Questions. Don't be afraid to ask your doctor about concerns you may have regarding your toddler's health and well-being.

103. Handling Doctor Visits

Here are some tips for making the most out of your doctor visits.

Make a list. Write down your questions ahead of time so you don't forget anything. Make sure you get the answers you need, but try not to waste your doctor's time with issues that could be resolved elsewhere.

Offer reminders. Make sure you bring up ongoing issues such as asthma, allergies, skin conditions, and other conditions your child might be dealing with. Also mention any medications your toddler is taking.

Take notes. Bring a notepad so you can jot things down in case you have a tendency to forget them when you get home.

Call back. If you forget something or don't understand instructions your doctor has given you, call the clinic when you get home. A nurse may be able to clarify the issue, or your doctor may call you back when he or she has time.

104. Doctor Visits: New Fears

Even after your toddler has visited the doctor regularly, she may suddenly develop a fear of the doctor, the office, or something related to the visit. If your toddler becomes upset about going to the doctor, here are tips that might help.

Fear of the unknown. Since your toddler may not remember what happens at the doctor visit, you can help ease her fears by telling her as much as you can about the upcoming visit. Remind her that though she may not remember them, she's had many good visits to the doctor's office.

Fear of separation. Your toddler may think she'll be separated from you in that strange place. Assure her that you will be with her all the time to protect her and comfort her.

Fear of pain. If your toddler is afraid to go to the doctor because she thinks she'll get a shot, reassure her that most visits don't involve shots. For ones that do, don't lie to her and tell her it won't hurt. Tell her you'll comfort her through the experience. You can also offer her a reward for being brave.

Fear of strangers. If your toddler hasn't been sick very often, the doctor may seem like a stranger. Or perhaps your toddler is anxious and afraid because she has a new doctor or because the clinic has new nurses and staff members. Be friendly toward the doctor and nurses to help ease your toddler's fear.

105. Medicine: It's *Not* Candy!

Part of keeping your toddler healthy involves handling her medicine. Here are some tips to help prevent mishaps with medication.

Lock it up. Keep all of your family's medications locked away or absolutely out of the reach of children.

Use child-resistant caps. Buy medicines with child-resistant caps and packaging, and make sure they're closed properly after each use.

Never call it "candy." You may be tempted to call medicine "candy" to entice your child to take it, but doing so is dangerous. If your child somehow finds a medicine bottle, she may be determined to have some more of that "candy."

Take it easy with vitamins. Be careful about giving your toddler too many vitamins; an overdose can be harmful. Talk to your doctor if you think a vitamin may be necessary.

Check the dosage. Make sure you measure the dosage precisely, and use the medication according to instructions on the bottle or from your doctor.

Use easy dispensers. Buy a child-appropriate medicine dispenser for an accurate measurement and easy dispensation.

Give one at a time. Don't give your toddler more than one medication (including both over-the-counter and prescription) without first checking with your doctor or pharmacist.

Throw it away. Discard medication after the expiration date has passed and dispose of the bottle. Always keep medications in their original containers.

Be careful. Never leave medicine unattended when you're giving it to your child.

106. Down the Hatch: Giving Medicine

Giving a toddler medicine isn't the easiest task, especially if she's picky about flavors, doesn't like to try new things, or is in a stubborn mood. Here are some tips for administering medicine to your toddler.

Be direct. Tell your toddler you're going to give her her medicine (remember, never call it "candy"). Talk to her about why the medicine is needed and how you hope it will help her.

Give her a preview. First pretend to give medicine to a doll to show your toddler how it will be done. On finishing, you might say, "That was a good job taking your medicine, Dolly!"

Get comfortable. Hold your toddler in your lap or in another comfortable position so she's relaxed and so you have better control over her than if she were standing. Do not have her lie on her back, which might cause choking.

Choose an appealing flavor. If available, choose a favorite or fun flavor for your toddler's medicine, such as cherry, grape, or bubble gum. If appropriate, request the flavor when your doctor writes the prescription.

Use a syringe. For easier administration, use a plastic syringe rather than a spoon. Measure the correct dose, insert the tip of the syringe between her lower side teeth and cheek, then squirt.

Offer a Popsicle. To numb your child's taste buds, let her suck on a Popsicle first. Then give her the medicine.

Disguise the medicine. If you have your doctor's approval, mix an unpalatable medicine with a small amount (1–2 teaspoons) of applesauce or fruit juice. Do not use larger amounts because the entire portion must be ingested.

Try other forms. If your toddler won't take liquid medicine, try chewable pills or easy-to-swallow capsules, if available. As a last resort, if your toddler just won't open her mouth, talk to your doctor about suppositories and shots.

Have a snack ready. After administering the medicine, give your toddler a snack (such as raisins, carrot sticks, peanut butter crackers, or juice) to take away any lingering bad taste.

Repeat, if necessary. If your toddler spits out or vomits the medicine, wait a few minutes and then administer a new dose.

107. Quick Tip: Disguise the Dose

Not only did my little girl refuse to take her medicine, she was also a picky eater. So it wasn't easy to sneak her medicine into her food. I finally tried mixing it with orange juice—and that did the trick. The flavor of the orange juice overpowered the taste of the medicine. I also served the juice in a small paper cup so it was fun and easy to drink. If your child doesn't like orange juice, try cranberry or apple juice. Just be sure all of it is finished.

—Barbara S.

Chapter 5
Toilet Training

108. Toilet Time

Attitudes toward toilet training have changed dramatically in the past few decades. In the past, parents began toilet training as early as 6 months. Over time, parents and child development experts realized most toddlers are not ready to toilet train until after two years of age. They need to be physically, cognitively, and psychologically ready for the experience. Here are some tips to help determine if your toddler is ready for toilet training.

Awareness. There are three general indicators of your child's readiness: (1) He's aware that he has wet or filled his diaper;(2) He's aware that he's in the process of wetting or filling his diaper; (3) He's aware that he's about to wet or fill his diaper. The higher the number, the greater the readiness.

Window of readiness. The majority of children display a window of readiness between the ages of 18 months and three years, depending on their maturity. Readiness depends not only on your child's individual maturation time, but also on his temperament and interest level.

Physical signs of readiness. Check to see if your toddler is more regular and predictable in his bowel movements, that he's staying dry during the day for longer periods of time, and that he's able to pull his pants down and pull them back up again.

Cognitive signs of readiness. Watch for signs that your toddler can follow simple instructions and understand the concept of learning to use the toilet. Also, notice whether he dislikes the feeling of being wet or soiled, and whether he can tell you that he's about to wet or fill his diaper.

Psychological signs of readiness. Assess your toddler's self-awareness, social awareness, general attitude toward things (positive or negative), and emotional readiness to train.

109. Signs That Your Child Is *Not* Ready

In addition to looking for signs of readiness, look for signs indicating that your child is not ready for toilet training.

Lack of awareness. Your toddler seems oblivious to the fact that he's wet or soiled, and he doesn't seem to sense when he's urinating or defecating.

No interest. Your toddler doesn't show any interest in his diaper, the potty-chair, the big toilet, or anything related to using the toilet.

Frequent urination. Your toddler wets his diaper every hour or two during the day. He probably isn't able to hold his urine long enough to toilet train.

Shows resistance. Your toddler resists your encouragement to try.

Stress. Your toddler is experiencing significant stress, such as moving to a new home, a death in the family, a new baby arriving, or a change in daycare.

Disability. Your toddler has a disability, such as a developmental delay or a physical handicap, which may slow the process.

110. Toilet Talk

The language you use to toilet train your child is important in helping him understand what's happening and what everything is called.

Use simple terms. Most experts recommend using simple terms for urination and defecation, such as *pee* and *poop.* Such terms are easier for your toddler to say, and they're more fun. There are other words to choose from, including *pee-pee, wee-wee,* and *tinkle* for urination, and *poo-poo, doo-doo, BM,* and *ca-ca* for bowel movements. Feel free to use other terms that have been used by your family. As your child gets older, you can begin using *urination* and *defecation,* if you like.

Avoid vague language. Some parents prefer less precise terms, such as *use the bathroom, go to the toilet,* or *make potty.* This is often done to avoid embarrassment in public or because parents are uncomfortable with more specific terminology. However, these terms may be confusing to your child, since they tend to be vague and unclear. It's better to use clear language (such as "it's time to try to pee in your potty" and "go to your potty and try to poop"), so your child knows exactly what you're talking about.

111. Types of Toilets

Here are the pros and cons for each toilet option.

Regular adult toilet. While the standard toilet may seem the most convenient tool for toilet training, it's designed for an adult's body, not a child's. It's large, uncomfortable, and intimidating to a small child. The loud flushing noise, the swirling water, and the mysterious objects that disappear into a seemingly black hole may frighten your child. Sitting on the big toilet can be precarious for an unsteady toddler who can't touch the floor with his feet. He may be afraid of falling off—or falling in.

Adapter seat. Adapter seats are designed to make the standard toilet more accommodating to a young child. The most common adapter seat is made of molded plastic shaped like a ring with a smaller opening to help your child sit more comfortably on the adult toilet. They're lightweight and portable, and there's no need for extra cleanup since you can simply flush the toilet after use. However, some adapter seat models can be a nuisance for adults since they have to be removed for adults' use and then replaced for a child's use. Some can also be uncomfortable and unsteady, and some may come loose from the toilet seat, causing the child to lose his balance and fall. If you choose an adapter seat, provide a stepstool or step-up ladder to help your child climb on more easily.

Potty-chair. Most children prefer the child-size potty-chair when they're just starting out. Potty-chairs help

make the experience less frightening, more pleasant, and a whole lot easier. They're appropriately designed for a small body, more comfortable than adapter seats, safe, and they don't produce any loud flushing noises or other frightening sounds. They can be moved from room to room for the convenience of both children and parents.

112. Toilet-Training Clothes

The clothes your toddler wears are crucial for helping him succeed at this important task. There are lots of options, including going naked.

Training pants. The most popular clothes for toilet training are pull-on training pants. They're elastic at the waist and easy for a toddler to pull up and down, which allows him to be more independent and more likely to get on the toilet or potty-chair on time.

Disposable versus cotton training pants. Disposable training pants are essentially thickly padded diapers that have an elastic waist and can be pulled on and off easily. Cotton training pants are underpants made with extra layers of cotton padding. You may want to begin with disposables, then change to cotton training pants.

Good supply. It's best to have about eight to ten pairs of training pants and regular underpants available at any given time during the toilet-training period.

Looser outer clothes. You might want to put your toddler in regular pants and shorts that are a little larger than normal, so they're easy to pull down and up but not so loose that they keep falling down.

Simple design. Avoid clothes with buckles, buttons, snaps, zippers, ties, belts, and other difficult fasteners. Avoid tights, overalls, and jump suits. Also avoid clothes that have to be tucked in, are layered, and are too long. Look for clothes with elastic waistbands, Velcro fasteners, short shirts, and other features that make them easy to get on and off.

No clothes? If you have a room with a washable floor and washable furniture (or a private yard), let your child go naked. Or he could just wear a short shirt and no pants or shoes (unless they are washable). Having a bare bottom is an excellent way to help your toddler be more aware of body signs of having to go. It's the easiest way, if you dare!

Big-kid underpants. When your child is ready for regular underpants, you might want to buy ones that are decorated with cartoon characters or special designs. These fancy prints make wearing underpants (or "big-kid pants") even more fun.

113. Toilet-Training Accessories

Here are some items (and ideas) you might want to have on hand when teaching your toddler how to use the toilet. They may help make the training experience more comfortable, pleasant, and fun.

Doll. Buy or borrow a doll that takes a bottle of water and then "wets." Include accessories such as baby bottles, training pants, and some clothes that are easily removed. Let your toddler train the doll while he learns to use the toilet. This will reinforce the process and help him feel in control.

Decorations. Personalize your child's potty-chair by attaching stickers and decals or by writing your toddler's name on it with a permanent marker.

Toilet paper fun. Show your toddler how much toilet paper to use by counting out a particular number of squares, by measuring an arm's length of paper, or by rolling out the paper until it touches the floor.

Targets. Boys sometimes enjoy aiming their urine flow at targets floating in the water. Plus, doing this helps their accuracy. You can buy paper submarines made for this purpose, or make your own targets from small pieces of paper, Cheerios, and so on.

Music. Consider using a cassette or CD player to play relaxing music while your toddler is using the potty.

Books. Keep a supply of picture books near the potty-chair for your child to look at while he sits. Having something to do can also relax him and keep him on the potty longer.

Toys. Keep a basket of toys within reach so your toddler can entertain himself while he sits. Make sure the toys are easy to handle, and wash them periodically to keep them germfree.

Rewards. Some parents like to reward their children with small candies, crackers, or stickers each time they successfully use the toilet. Others use a chart to mark successes as they happen, then reward with a toy or snack at the end of the day or week. Remember, your words of encouragement and approval are the most effective reward you can give your child.

114. Find the Right Time to Begin

Selecting the right time to begin toilet training may be important to success. Not only do you want to make sure your child is ready physically, cognitively, and emotionally, you also want to choose the most favorable time.

Season. Summer is usually the best season to begin since your child is wearing just a few lightweight clothes (or nothing at all, weather permitting). This makes getting on the toilet on time much easier.

Vacation week. You might consider using at-home vacation time to begin toilet training your toddler. Avoid beginning toilet training when you're on a traveling vacation.

Weekend. Consider using a long weekend. Devote each day to playing with your child in a relaxed way, while at the same time observing him and his cues that he might be ready to go. Pick a weekend when you'll have no expected visitors, no appointments, and no errands to run. Just focus on playing, eating, and toilet training with as few interruptions as possible.

Time of day. Some children are more alert in the morning, while others do better in the afternoon. Try to begin toilet training when your toddler is most alert and energetic.

Follow his habits. Your toddler's elimination habits may help determine your toilet-training schedule. For example, many children void their bladder or bowels after mealtime, while others need to go first thing in the morning or after naptime.

115. Taking the First Steps

Here are some tips for getting things underway.

Dress your child in transition pants. Start the process by changing your toddler into transition pants—either pull-up diapers or padded cotton training pants. Let him practice pulling the transition pants up and down.

Watch for cues. Keep an eye out for signs that your toddler needs to use the toilet. Then escort him to the potty-chair quickly and calmly.

Choose regular times. If your child urinates or defecates at certain times during the day, head for the potty-chair at those times.

Motivate your child. If your child is reluctant to try the potty-chair, you might want to motivate him with small rewards for each step he takes, such as a sticker if he pulls down his own pants or a small fruit candy if he sits on the toilet.

Praise the progress. Again, your smiling face, clapping hands, and proud words are the most important rewards you can provide.

Use potty prompts. Remind your child about the potty every so often by saying, "Do you need to pee or poop in your potty?" or "Let's remember to use the potty when we need to pee or poop."

Supervision. Always keep an eye on your child while he's on the toilet.

116. Quick Tip: Getting Started

We set the potty-chair in the bathroom for a couple of weeks so our daughter could get used to seeing it without any pressure. We talked about its purpose, compared it to the big toilet, and told her the potty-chair was her very own. We told her that when she was ready, she could learn how to use it. When she first tried, she clearly didn't like the idea, so we stopped for a week or two. When she tried again, she had immediate success. I think children need to get used to new things without feeling pressured to accept them. A positive attitude is the key to success. If it isn't a big deal for parents, it won't be for kids either.

—Gay C.

117. Quick Tip: Show and Tell

Model the behavior you want by showing your child how you use the toilet. Leave the door open and let him see you, or invite him in if he's interested. Let him sit on his potty-chair while you sit on the big toilet. Don't make a big deal of it. Remain casual so your child will feel the same way. Make sure both parents get a chance to demonstrate using the toilet in a straightforward way.

—Shi P.

118. Following Up

Now that you've officially started the lessons, it's important to follow through with prompts, practice, praise, and rewards.

Make frequent visits. Remind your toddler to sit on the toilet once every hour or so. Sitting on the potty-chair may become a trigger that helps him release his urine and BMs.

Offer reminders. Your toddler may become so engaged in play that he loses his potty awareness and forgets to go. Remind him every so often, but don't irritate him with constant interruptions.

Expect accidents. It takes time to learn a new task, especially at a young age. There will be accidents, so take them in stride. Don't make a fuss about them, or your child may become inhibited or feel like a failure. Make a nonjudgmental comment, clean up together, and move on.

Continue praising and rewarding. Don't let up on the positive reinforcement. Keep telling your child that he's done a good job and that you're proud of him for trying. If he needs additional motivators, try a special activity or small new toy when he's stayed dry all day.

119. Basic Maintenance

Here are some maintenance tips to consider during toilet-training lessons.

Quick cleanup. Pour a little water into the bottom of the potty bowl to make cleanup easier.

Toilet paper. As needed, remind your toddler how much toilet paper to use, such as an arm's length, four to six squares, or until the paper reaches the floor.

Wiping. Make sure your toddler wipes from front to back to prevent a possible urinary tract infection.

Paper only. Let your toddler know that, apart from urine and BMs, only toilet paper goes in the toilet. Tell him if he puts toys or other objects into the toilet, it may clog and overflow. If necessary, keep a childproof lock on the toilet to avoid problems.

Flushing fascination. Talk about where urine and feces go, where the water comes from, what causes the flushing, and other details about the toilet. Many toddlers are fascinated by how toilets work. If your child seems wary of flushing or using the big toilet, don't push it. Let him warm up on his own.

Fun soap. To encourage your child to wash his hands, provide fun bars of soap in cartoon designs or creative shapes, or use liquid soap in a bottle that has bright designs on it.

Stepstool. Provide a step-stool so your toddler can reach the adult toilet when he's ready to try. The step-stool will also help your child reach the light switch and the sink for hand washing.

120. Genital Play

During toilet-training time, many toddlers—both boys and girls—rediscover their genitals and play with them. This can be disconcerting to parents, but it's entirely normal. Here are some tips for coping with this curiosity.

Private time. Allow your toddler some time to be alone and to explore his body if he wants to. You can give him private time while he's lying in his bed, or you can let him enjoy some naked time after a bath. Let him know that certain behavior is not acceptable in public, however.

No shame. Don't tell your toddler he's doing something wrong. He's simply exploring his body parts. You don't want him to feel ashamed about his body, which could damage his self-image. Don't make a big deal of this normal stage of development. It will pass without your intervention.

Appropriate words. When you talk about your toddler's body, use normal vocabulary such as *penis* or *vagina*. If you're already using certain terms as part of your toilet-training terminology, it's okay to continue using them. However, try to avoid disparaging or unclear terms such *wiener* or *down there*. Don't be embarrassed when talking to your child about his genitals; they're simply a part of his body.

121. Toilet-Training Concerns

While toilet training goes smoothly for most children, some kids encounter problems that delay or interfere with the process. Here are some typical concerns and tips for dealing with them.

Offer more reminders. If your toddler has trouble staying dry, you might need to check him more frequently and remind him more often to use the toilet.

Change trainers. If your toddler seems to be in a power struggle with you, have your partner do the training for a change.

Change sites. If your toddler doesn't seem to like the room where you've placed the potty-chair, move it to a new room. If you're playing outside with your toddler, bring the potty-chair outside with you.

Increase rewards. If your toddler doesn't seem sufficiently motivated, increase the rewards. Then gradually wean him from the rewards.

Give choices. If your toddler always says "no" to your reminders and prompts, give him choices such as, "Do you want to try the potty *before* lunch or *after* lunch?"

Increase liquids. If your toddler doesn't seem to have to go very often, increase his liquid intake during the training period.

122. Special Concerns

Some toddlers are toilet trained by age three; others need another six months to a year to complete the training. Your child may experience a few setbacks, accidents, or digressions along the way. Here are some tips for managing problems.

Fears. Some children begin to fear the toilet, even after they've been using it for some time. Reassure your toddler that he's doing well, that the toilet is safe, and that you're proud of his progress. Stick with the potty-chair as long as he needs it to feel secure.

Distractions. If something new happens in your toddler's life, such as a move, a divorce, or a new baby, he may become reluctant to use the toilet or may wet himself by accident more often. Be sure to be attentive, supportive, and calm, and carry on the training as best you can. If necessary, suspend training until things settle down.

Negativity. Some toddlers remain in the negative stage longer and rebel at the toilet-training process for seemingly no reason. Try to stay positive and offer rewards for your child's progress. Or set aside toilet training until he's in a more cooperative stage.

Real problems. If your toddler is having real problems urinating or defecating, have your doctor do a thorough checkup to make sure nothing's wrong.

123. *Quick Tip: Holding BMs*

My toddler often strained and cried when he had a bowel movement. When I realized he was holding back his bowel movements, I called his doctor. She recommended giving him more liquids, fruit, and a high-fiber diet as a natural laxative. She also suggested I read to him while he was on the toilet to help him relax. After about a week of this regimen, our problem was solved.

—Mary W.

124. *Quick Tip: Sneaky Stuff*

The biggest problem for me was getting my daughter to go to the toilet when she didn't really have to go, such as before a long car trip or before bedtime or naptime. This would always end up in a power struggle. So finally I told her that sometimes pee-pee is sneaky. It hides until you don't have a toilet around, then it wants to come out. If you don't get it out ahead of time, it will sneak out—and then you're out of luck. So I encouraged her to get on the potty and tell that pee-pee to GET OUT OF THERE! It worked beautifully!

—Kelly S.

125. Switching to the Big Toilet

If your toddler has used the potty-chair successfully for some time, he may be ready to switch to the big toilet. Here are some tips for making the transition.

Readiness. If your toddler manages his clothing easily, uses the potty-chair well, and doesn't have many accidents, he's probably ready for the big toilet. If he has trouble in any of those areas, give him a little more time.

Preparation. Talk about the big toilet before you make the switch. Discuss how it's similar to the potty-chair, what he needs to do to use it successfully, and why he will want to try the big toilet.

Stepstool. Provide a small stepstool so your toddler can reach the big toilet easily and safely. Decorate it with stickers and write your toddler's name on it, then let him practice stepping up and down before he tries the big toilet.

Practice. Have your toddler try sitting on the big toilet with his pants up, just to get a feel for it. The toilet is less likely to be intimidating if your toddler gets a chance to test it without any pressure.

Go! When you think your toddler is ready to try the big toilet, tell him he can use it next time. Or, better yet, have him try before he has to go urgently, so he can take his time

126. Staying Dry Overnight

Most children aren't able to stay dry all night until they're four to six years old. For some children, learning to stay dry overnight happens soon after daytime dryness. If you think your toddler is ready to give it a try, here are some helpful hints.

Prepare the bed. Line the bed with a plastic cover to help keep the mattress dry if your toddler wets the bed.

Use thicker pants. Buy thicker pants to help absorb any accidents.

Control liquid intake. Cut down on fluids between dinnertime and bedtime.

Make one last trip. Just before your toddler goes to bed, have him sit on the toilet one last time.

Get up during the night. Some children can be gently roused during the night for a potty visit. Others may need to call out during the night to have you help them use the bathroom.

Go first thing in the morning. When your toddler wakes up in the morning, remind him to go to the potty first thing.

Offer praise. When your toddler stays dry all night, give him lots of praise. If he doesn't, tell him it's okay and that he can try again next time.

127. Travel Tips

Traveling with your toddler may interfere with his toilet-training progress, but if you're prepared, you can minimize many problems.

Go before you go. Have your toddler go before you leave, so he's less likely to have to go while in the car.

Bring a porta-potty. Bring along a porta-potty so your child has a familiar place to go, if he needs that.

Bring wipes. Bring toilet paper, tissues, or wipes so your toddler can clean himself after he goes.

Take breaks. Make frequent stops along the way and have your toddler try to go.

Bring clothes. Pack extra underpants, pants, shoes, and socks in case of an accident.

No toilet, no problem. If there's no toilet nearby and your toddler has to go, let him urinate outdoors in a safe, out-of-the-way place. This isn't something you want to encourage, but it is kind of fun when you're in a pinch! Or bring along an extra pull-up diaper and have him go in that. Then wipe him and put his underpants back on.

128. Check with Your Doctor

If you have any concerns that your toddler's toilet training may not be proceeding normally, talk to your doctor. Here are some signs to watch for.

- Your child hasn't had a bowel movement in three days.
- Your child hasn't urinated in twelve hours or is going infrequently (every four hours) with low urine output.
- Your child urinates very frequently (every half hour).
- Your child strains when urinating or defecating.
- Your child experiences pain when urinating or defecating.
- Your child uses the toilet but also wets his underwear frequently (every other time).
- Your child is over four and still isn't toilet trained.
- You suspect something is wrong with your child's ability to toilet train.

Chapter 6
Safety

129. Emergency Basics

As much as we try to avoid them, accidents and emergencies happen. Here are the basics you need to know in case of a medical emergency.

Phone numbers. Keep emergency numbers handy at all times, wherever you are. (See Tip 129.)

First-aid kit. Prepare a first-aid kit (or two) for emergencies, and keep them handy in your home and vehicle. (See Tip 135.)

CPR. Make sure you know how to administer age-appropriate cardiopulmonary resuscitation (CPR). Classes with hands-on practice are often available at community education centers and schools. Otherwise, see "Rescue breathing (CPR)" in Tip 135.

Help. If possible, get help from a neighbor or nearby relative so you can make phone calls or other arrangements or so you can focus solely on comforting and caring for your toddler.

130. Emergency Numbers

Make at least two copies of a list of emergency numbers, and keep them handy—for example, keep one next to the phone in your house and another in your wallet. You need to have quick and easy access to these numbers at all times. Here are some important numbers to keep on hand.

- 911 for police, fire department, and medical assistance (including ambulance)
- Poison control (Poison Help at 1-800-222-1222)
- Hospital emergency room
- Pediatrician, family doctor, or clinic
- Reliable neighbors
- You and your partner's work numbers
- Pediatric dentist
- Relatives
- Daycare contacts

131. Quick Tip: Poison Control Number

Keep the poison control number handy. But if you suspect your child has ingested something potentially harmful and you don't have the poison control number at your fingertips, don't waste time looking for it. Call 911 and the dispatcher will transfer you to poison control. Time is critical.

—Dana M.

132. Poison Awareness

You may not be aware of it, but there are poisons lurking in many areas of your home, garage, and yard. Here's a list of some of the common hazards.

- Air fresheners
- Alcohol
- Batteries
- Bleach
- Cigarettes
- Cleansers
- Cosmetics
- Detergents
- Disinfectants
- Drain cleaners
- Dyes
- Fabric softeners
- Fertilizers
- Floor cleaners
- Gasoline
- Insect repellent
- Laundry products
- Lighter fluid
- Lotions
- Matches
- Mothballs
- Paints
- Pen ink
- Pencil lead
- Pesticides
- Plants (some)
- Shampoos
- Stain removers
- Starch
- Toothpaste

133. Prevent Choking

Some toddlers will put just about anything in their mouths, including foods and objects that might cause choking. Since choking can lead to a life-threatening situation, here are some tips to avoid it.

Remove hazards. Periodically inspect your toddler's play area and the rest of your home. Remove any items that could be choking hazards. (See Tips 134 and 135.)

Watch out. Remember to keep an especially close eye on your toddler when you're in an environment where choking hazards may be present.

No running. Be sure your toddler sits down while she eats (and be sure her food is cut into small pieces).

134. Choking Hazards: Foods

Here are some common foods that are choking hazards.

- Small, hard candies
- Carrots and other hard vegetables
- Celery and other stringy foods
- Cheese cubes
- Grapes, cherries, and apple chunks
- Gum
- Hot dogs (circular slices)
- Meat chunks
- Peanut butter and other sticky foods
- Peanuts and other nuts
- Popcorn
- Raisins (too many at once)

135. Choking Hazards: Household Items

Here are some household items that are choking hazards.

- Balloons
- Small, round batteries
- Buttons
- Coins
- Erasers
- Jewelry
- Marbles
- Marker caps
- Nails, tacks, and screws
- Plastic bags
- Safety pins, straight pins
- Small balls
- Small toys and toy parts

136. Choking: What to Do

Assess. If your toddler is choking, first determine if she can speak or cough. If so, let her try to cough up the object on her own. If she can't, look into her mouth and see if you can identify the object. Don't blindly sweep the mouth or you may push the object farther down. If you can see the object, use your fingers to pull it out carefully.

Respond. If you can't remove the object, do abdominal thrusts (Heimlich maneuver) modified for toddlers. Stand or kneel behind your child, and wrap your arms around her chest. Place a fist against the middle of her abdomen. Press into the abdomen with quick upward thrusts until she coughs up the object.

Rescue breathing (CPR). If your toddler is unconscious and not breathing, have someone call 911. Continue to try to remove the object, then begin rescue breathing. Lay your child on her back, lift her chin, pinch her nose, and seal your lips over her mouth. Give one breath every three seconds for one minute, then check to see if there's a pulse. If not, do 1-inch-deep chest compressions with the heel of one hand on your child's sternum at a rate of one hundred per minute. That's about twenty-five compressions every fifteen seconds. Give one mouth-to-mouth breath for every five compressions.

137. First-Aid Kit

It's always a good idea to keep a first-aid kit handy—especially with an accident-prone toddler around the house. Here are some items to include.

- Acetaminophen (Tylenol)
- Adhesive tape
- Antibacterial cream
- Antiseptic liquid soap
- Antiseptic spray
- Band-Aids
- Calamine lotion
- Cotton
- First-aid guide, including CPR instructions
- Ice pack
- Medicine dispenser
- Needle
- Rubbing alcohol
- Scissors
- Sterile pads
- Syrup of ipecac
- Teething medication
- Thermometer
- Tweezers

138. Treating Owies

If your toddler does hurt herself—and no doubt she will at some point—here are some tips for treating minor injuries.

Cuts and scrapes. Hold the injured area under cool water for a few minutes, and wash it gently with mild soap. Apply a nonstinging antibiotic and cover the area with a bandage. Call your doctor if the bleeding doesn't stop in five minutes or if the injury doesn't improve in a few days.

Bruises and sore muscles. Apply an ice pack (or towel-covered bag of frozen vegetables) to the area for fifteen minutes. Wait thirty minutes and repeat. Call your doctor if there's stiffness or if the area can't take any pressure.

Smashed fingers. Apply an ice pack to prevent swelling, and hold the hand above your child's heart. Call your doctor if you think the finger is broken or if the nail is bloody or loose. If any skin is broken, use the same treatment as for cuts and scrapes, above.

Nosebleeds. Have your toddler lean slightly forward while you squeeze the front of her nose for five minutes. If the bleeding continues, hold the nose for another ten minutes. Call your doctor if you suspect the nose is broken or if the bleeding continues after fifteen minutes.

Stingers, ticks, and splinters. Remove the item carefully with tweezers or your fingernails, wash the area with soap and water, and apply an antiseptic. Call your doctor or nurse if you cannot remove the stinger or tick. Call also if a rash or infection develops.

139. Quick Tip: Bite Your Tongue

If my child falls down, I try to avoid crying out "oh, no!" or otherwise overreacting. I wait just a few seconds to see if he's really hurt. He may not cry unless he's scared by my loud, worried reaction. If he's got a little owie, I always give it a kiss and sometimes apply a cartoon Band-Aid. They always seem to do the trick.

—*Susan W.*

140. Quick Tip: Doctoring a Doll

Whenever my daughter got sick or had a boo-boo, I'd take care of her first, and then I'd give her a doll so she could make it feel better, too. She'd take the doll's temperature, put Band-Aids on it, rock it, and do whatever she thought it needed. Later, I even bought her a little toy medical kit. It was a great way for her to forget her own ailments and express her feelings.

—*Eric G.*

141. Preventing Accidents and Injuries

The best way to prevent accidents and injuries, of course, is to supervise your toddler at all times. It only takes a second for her to get into dangerous situations. Always know where she is and keep her in sight as much as possible. Here are six other fundamental tips for preventing accidents and injuries.

1. Lock up poisons, medicines, and dangerous chemicals.

2. Avoid storing guns in your home. If you do, use gunlocks and keep the weapons in a locked cabinet. Store ammunition in a separate locked location.

3. Never hit, shake, drag by the arm, or play too rough with your toddler.

4. Don't expose your child to domestic violence.

5. Toddler-proof your home and yard. (See Tips 148–156.)

6. Always use a government-approved safety seat for your toddler when traveling by car. The safety seat is necessary until she weighs forty pounds; then use a booster seat. (See Tip 350.)

142. *Quick Tip: Purse Play*

My toddler was fascinated by my purse. When she wasn't carrying it around, she was dumping the contents on the floor and exploring everything. Since there were lots of things inside that weren't safe—coins, pens, medications—I really had to keep an eye on her. One day I caught her in my purse about to eat my ChapStick. I went out that day and bought her a small purse that looked like mine. Together we found things to put inside that were fun and safe, such as toy keys, a plastic wallet, play money, a bag of snacks, a washable marker, and so on. She loved having her own purse. From that day on I kept my own purse in a safe place when it wasn't with me.

—Mariah N.

143. *Quick Tip: Prevention Pays*

It's good to instruct (and remind) babysitters and other care providers to be extra observant around your toddler. They may not be as diligent as you in keeping tabs on his whereabouts and in anticipating safety issues. You know what they say about an ounce of prevention.... If something does happen, try not to blame anyone. Learn from the mistake and try to ensure it never happens again.

—Susan W.

144. Keeping Your Toddler Safe

Curious and speedy toddlers want to explore almost everything they can get their hands on. While that's great for physical and cognitive development, it sometimes means she will get into trouble before you know it. Here are tips to help keep your active toddler safe during these busy years.

Anticipate. When your toddler wants to play with something potentially dangerous, anticipate the possible ways she could be injured. If other children are playing near your child, anticipate their behavior and how it may affect her. Closely supervise your child's play in circumstances such as these and be ready to intervene if necessary.

Point out certain dangers. Introduce your toddler to some of the dangers in her environment. You don't want to scare her into being overly timid, but you do want her to know about certain dangers, such as hot surfaces, sharp objects, and so on.

Warn your child. Especially if your toddler has high energy, she's apt to try things that may cause injury—for example, jumping down a few stairs. Talk to her about potential dangers, but again, don't scare her. Use simple, clear language to explain the threats.

145. Quick Tip: Climbing Cautiously

While my toddler was learning to walk, he also began trying to climb almost everything—some were safe ventures, but others weren't. Too many times I had to rescue him from big falls, and I knew I had to teach him to be cautious. For the next few weeks, each time he started to climb, I said, "Always stay by Mommy when you're climbing!" Then when the situation called for it, I added stern warnings about the dangers of unstable structures and climbing too high. After a few more tumbles and my repeated warnings, he did become more cautious and wasn't so eager to climb without my presence.

—Sara Lynn D.

146. Quick Tip: Hot Coffee

One danger I hadn't thought about was right in front of my face—hot coffee. I drink a lot of coffee during the day, and one time I left the mug where my toddler could reach it. If I hadn't walked in just as she was reaching for it, she would have pulled the whole cup down on herself. Now I make a point to be very aware of where my daughter—and my coffee—is.

—Sujata M.

147. Lost Child

Toddlers sometimes inadvertently walk away from parents or caregivers. Here are some tips for keeping your toddler safe while you're out and about.

Keep a watchful eye. Always keep an eye on your toddler. She's curious, mobile, and eager to explore her independence—and she can slip away from you before you know it. Never assume she's at your side; always check to make sure she's near you.

Teach safety. Your toddler isn't too young to learn some simple safety measures. Remind her to stay with you at all times, teach her her full name, and—when she is ready—start teaching her her phone number and address.

Alert others. As soon as you discover your toddler is lost, immediately alert any staff, security, and people nearby. The sooner you announce that your child is lost, the sooner you'll find her.

Carry pictures. Always have a picture of your toddler on hand so you can show it to people who may have seen her.

Call your child's name. Don't hesitate to call out your toddler's name while you're looking for her. This is not the time to be quiet and shy. If there's a public address system available, use that, too.

148. Toddler-Proofing Basics

Now that your toddler is moving, toddler-proof your home to make sure she stays safe. Here are some tips for preventing accidents and injuries.

Drapery cords. Make sure the cords are out of your child's reach or tied up so your toddler can't choke on them.

Electrical outlets. Put plastic plugs in outlets and sockets to keep your toddler from inserting her fingers or other items.

Electrical cords. Tuck electrical cords under carpets and furniture, or cover them with duct tape so your toddler won't trip or chew on them.

Sharp corners. Use plastic covers or padding to cover sharp corners and edges on coffee tables and other items so your toddler won't injure her head if she falls nearby.

Rugs. Make sure slippery rugs are secure or remove them to prevent slipping, tripping, or falling.

Windows. Keep all windows locked as much as possible. When windows (especially those on a second floor) are open, place bars or gates over them to insure your toddler doesn't fall out.

Stairs. If you have a two-story house, put gates at both the top and bottom of the stairs to prevent your toddler from tumbling down.

Poisonous plants. Call poison control to see if any of your houseplants—which could include daffodils, poinsettias, and azaleas—are poisonous, and remove those that are.

Smoke detectors. Install smoke detectors on every floor in your home. Test the batteries every few months. Keep a fire extinguisher in the kitchen (out of reach of your toddler). Plan escape routes in case of fire.

Off-limits. Use gates or plastic doorknob covers to keep your toddler out of off-limits rooms.

149. Quick Tip: Visiting Friends

When you take your toddler to a friend's home, be aware that their house may not be childproofed. You'll have to keep an eye on your child at all times.

—Karen M.

150. Quick Tip: Babysitter Safety

When I get a new babysitter for my kids, I always have her come over a half hour early so I can take her on a safety tour of my house. I show her all the possible dangers, what I've done to childproof, and where all the emergency numbers are. Then I ask her some basic questions such as, "What would you do in case of an emergency?" "Do you know

how to operate a fire extinguisher?" and so on. I just don't feel comfortable if a babysitter isn't prepared to deal with emergencies.

—Susan A.

151. Toddler-Proofing the Kitchen

One of the most dangerous rooms in the house is the kitchen. Here are some tips to make sure your kitchen is safe for your toddler.

Appliances. Make sure unused appliances are unplugged and kept out of reach of toddlers.

Stove. Keep your toddler away from the hot stove when you're cooking, and never leave the oven door open. Turn pot handles away from the front of the stove so your toddler can't grab them.

Sink. Don't let your toddler play with the faucets, and set your water heat at 120°F or lower to avoid scalding.

Knives. Store knives and other dangerous kitchen equipment in locked cabinets or toddler-proofed drawers.

Cleaning substances. Keep cleansers, chemicals, and other cleaning supplies out of reach or locked securely in cabinets.

Garbage. Keep garbage in a locked container or cabinet so your toddler can't get into it.

Plastic bags. Keep new and used plastic bags out of reach. There is a danger of suffocation if your toddler puts one over her head.

152. Quick Tip: Dangerous Distractions

Be careful about dishwashing detergent. I filled the little holder, turned to answer the phone, and came back to find my toddler feasting on the stuff. Some of these detergents contain lye and other ingredients dangerous to kids. You should never turn your back on your toddler when unsafe items are nearby.

—Anne G.

153. Quick Tip: Trash It

Watch out for garbage! My son got into the trash once while I was getting the mail, and he had it all over the floor. It looked like he'd been eating coffee grounds, so I took him to the doctor. When I got home, I put a lock on the garbage cupboard.

—Sally F.

154. Toddler-Proofing the Bathroom

Usually the second-most dangerous room in your house is your bathroom. Here are some tips for making sure it's safe for your toddler.

Door. Place plastic doorknob covers on bathroom doors, and keep the doors shut so your toddler can't go into the room without your supervision.

Water temperature. Again, set the water heater at 120°F or lower to prevent your toddler from being scalded.

Bathtub. Put a rubber mat or thick plastic stickers on the floor of the tub to prevent slipping. Never leave your toddler unattended in the bathtub, not even for a moment.

Toilet. Attach a safety lock to your toilet seat so your toddler doesn't fall in and drown.

Appliances. Keep hair dryers, radios, and other electrical items out of reach in the bathroom.

Chemicals. Lock up shampoos, soaps, cosmetics, perfumes, hair products, and anything else that could be dangerous if ingested.

Medicines. Lock up all your medicines and keep them out of reach. Always request safety caps when filling prescriptions.

155. Toddler-Proofing Your Child's Room

Although your toddler's room should be the safest place in your home, there are hazards you need to be aware of.

Crib. Make sure your toddler's crib was never painted with lead paint and that the slats are narrow enough (2⅜ inches apart) so she can't fit her head through the openings. Don't place the crib near a window or shelf.

Changing table. Be sure your changing table is sturdy enough that it won't tip over while you're changing your ever-growing toddler. Keep changing supplies out of reach when you're not using them.

Toy chest. Check the lid and hinges on the toy chest to make sure the lid won't come crashing down, which might trap your toddler inside or smash her fingers. Remove or disable any latches or locks so your toddler can't lock herself in. Make sure there are plenty of air holes in case she does crawl in and lower the lid. Better yet, remove the lid.

Toys. Initially, be sure your toddler's toys are safe, nontoxic, and age appropriate. Check frequently for broken parts that might have sharp edges. Also, as your toddler's cognitive skills increase, she may explore or use her toys in new ways. What might seem like a safe toy may become a problem if she tries to use it inappropriately. For example, she might use a toy drumstick to poke the family pet, or she might rip open a covering on a toy and find a tightly coiled, sharp spring. You'll need to supervise her play even more closely if such incidents arise.

156. Quick Tip: Crib Cover

There's a product on the market that prevents toddlers from falling out of their cribs. It's a see-through structure that resembles a tent and is installed over the crib. Kids think it's cool, kind of like a fort! It also keeps them from climbing out.

—Anne G.

Chapter 7
Discipline

157. Basic Dos and Don'ts

Setting limits or rules for a toddler's behavior is an emotional and personal issue for nearly all parents. Whatever your style, here are a few general guidelines to keep in mind.

Model the behaviors you value. Your toddler learns mostly from what you do and don't do. Be mostly cheerful and cooperative, not grouchy and stubborn. Respect other people's feelings and property.

Avoid the behaviors you don't like. For example, never hit anyone. Don't shout, yell, or scream. Avoid taking dangerous or unnecessary risks. Don't ridicule others.

Know your toddler's "stage." By understanding your toddler's developmental stage, you'll know that some undesired behaviors, such as saying "no" and being negative (see Tip 170), are normal.

Be aware of impulsive behavior. Much of a toddler's behavior—such as singing, hugging, jumping, pushing, hitting, having a tantrum—is impulsive. He doesn't plan to behave or misbehave; at times he simply can't control his behavior. He will, however, slowly develop the ability to control his impulses.

Be patient. Teaching your child appropriate behavior takes time; it doesn't happen overnight. Your toddler will need lots of repetition in order to learn a lesson and begin to change his behavior.

158. Discipline Styles

Child development experts have found that parenting styles usually fall into one of three categories. Here are the most common parenting styles and how they affect a child.

Permissive parent. The permissive parent generally lacks or chooses not to use discipline techniques. He or she lets the child do whatever he likes, thinking he will learn from the consequences of his behavior. The child has no set bedtime, no rules, and no real guidance. Children of permissive parents tend to lack self-guidance and rarely learn from their behavior—usually because no one is really teaching them anything.

Authoritarian parent. The authoritarian parent tends to be the opposite of the permissive parent. The word of the authoritarian parent is law, and the child is not free to negotiate the situation. The child must do as he is told, without question. Children of authoritarian parents also tend to lack self-guidance because they don't get the opportunity to think for themselves or to learn from trial and error.

Democratic-authoritative parent. The democratic-authoritative parent is willing to listen to his or her child and negotiate the situation, but retains the final say. Children of democratic parents tend to have greater self-esteem, self-help skills, self-guidance, and self-confidence, because they learn how to deal with situations under the guidance of an experienced parent.

159. Teaching and Guiding

While some parents immediately think of discipline as punishment, most child development experts see discipline as an opportunity to teach. Your ultimate goal is to help your toddler develop self-control and a sense of appropriate behavior.

Offer explanations. Don't just tell your toddler what to do or what not to do. Explain in simple terms why you want him to do certain things and not to do others. If he's done something you don't like, talk about how he can change his behavior next time.

Grab teaching opportunities. On the ride to the library, talk about why he'll need to use a soft voice and not run. When you're eating a meal with your toddler, introduce one or two table manners. When you're expecting guests, explain the social behaviors you like and those you don't.

Be consistent. Set clear limits and follow through consistently so your toddler knows he has boundaries. He'll test them to make sure they're real, but consistent limits will actually help him feel more secure in the long run. Changing your mind or giving in confuses a toddler.

Redirect. Sometimes it's best to redirect your toddler's attention away from a problem and toward a more constructive activity. For example, if he's scaring a younger sibling or a friend, let him make funny and scary faces in a mirror. If he's roughhousing in the family room, take him outside to play ball or otherwise work off excess energy.

Acknowledge his temperament. No two toddlers are exactly alike, nor is your toddler exactly the same one moment to the next. Study your child's temperament, emotions, and energy levels throughout the day, and modify your teaching and guiding techniques accordingly.

Say "no" sparingly. Use "no" only when you really need it. Overusing it often diminishes its effectiveness. When you do use it, make sure your body language and tone of voice match the word, but avoid scaring your child. If you say "no" tentatively or unconvincingly, your child may become confused or may simply ignore you.

Arrange success. Show your toddler how to do something positive and appropriate. For example, show him how to put away his toys gently instead of throwing them. Do it together, praising him when he does it.

Use natural consequences. Whenever possible, allow your toddler to learn a lesson through natural consequences. For example, say he breaks a toy by abusing it. Explain to him it can no longer be used because he chose to play with it too roughly. Then remove the toy.

Explain his options. If you can't allow a natural consequence because of safety, financial, or other reasons, warn your toddler of the consequences of his inappropriate behavior. For example, tell him if he gets his new shoes dirty, he'll have to wear his old shoes—or his dirty shoes—to his friend's birthday party.

160. Quick Tip: Give Reasons

When I say "no" to my son, I tell him why in simple terms so he understands my decisions aren't arbitrary. I've discovered that if I tell him the truth about why something's dangerous or why he needs to put away his toys, he's more inclined to cooperate. I do the same when I say "yes" so he knows there are reasons when I say "yes," too.

—Susan W.

161. Quick Tip: Timer Trick

My son was a classic dawdler. A friend recommended that I use a timer to keep him moving. I thought this might upset him since he already had a problem with time. But I decided to try it. I set the timer for two minutes and encouraged him to get his socks on before the bell rang! He had so much fun beating the timer that he carried it with him and tried to beat the bell with almost everything he did. When the fascination wore off, I noticed his dawdling had decreased, too.

—Nancy K.

162. Set Up a Positive Environment

One of the easiest ways to prevent behavior problems is to set up a positive environment for your toddler. Offer your toddler opportunities to explore and play without putting himself in danger or trouble. Here are some tips for setting up a toddler-friendly environment.

Make it safe. Make your toddler's play area safe and accessible. Minimize potential problems by removing dangerous, expensive, or breakable items or by putting them out of reach. (See Tips 148–156.)

Limit access. Put up gates or close doors on stairways and other off-limits areas. That way your toddler won't be able to get into harmful situations, and you won't have to worry about it.

Offer fun. Make sure your toddler has lots of fun things to play with so he's interested and occupied. Otherwise he'll be tempted to get into things that aren't appropriate.

Supervise. Even though the environment should do most of the work, don't leave your toddler unattended for long periods of time. Keep an eye on him so you can intervene if he gets into trouble.

163. Nonnegotiable Areas

Experts believe setting limits is crucial for effective discipline. Here are three key areas where you should not be willing to compromise.

Respect self. Teach your toddler to respect himself. Help your toddler know he's important by doing your best to take care of him and his needs. Teach him how to stay out of danger, appreciate his abilities, and take care of his own needs, as he is able.

Respect others. Your toddler should not be allowed to cause deliberate harm to other people. Teach him not to hurt others by modeling respectful and polite behavior and by explaining how it feels to be the other person.

Respect property. Your toddler must learn to be careful with other people's things. He also must learn to look after his own things. Teach him how to be gentle with his toys, other children's toys, household objects, and other property. If he accidentally breaks something, help him fix it, if possible.

164. Quick Tip: Respect

To discipline means to teach, and the best thing you can teach your child is respect. If you teach your child respect, you'll eliminate many problems.

—Susan W

165. No Spanking

Most experts and parents alike consider spanking an inappropriate, ineffective, and unnecessary form of discipline. Here's why.

Spanking frightens children. Imagine a towering giant reaching down and striking you! That's how a toddler feels when being hit by a parent. When you hit your child, you're not really teaching him anything except fear.

Spanking breaks down trust. A toddler is powerless when spanked by a parent. Any trust the child might have had in the parent is shaken.

Spanking doesn't work. Scaring your child into submission might deter the behavior in the short run. But it doesn't teach your child why the behavior is unacceptable, what the appropriate behavior is, or how he can change his behavior.

Spanking teaches negative behaviors. Spanking teaches negative behaviors, such as aggression and violence, instead of positive behaviors, such as self-control, problem solving, and empathy.

Spanking is dangerous. Child development experts agree that spanking can damage a child physically, psychologically, and emotionally. Experts also have shown that spanking can easily escalate into child abuse. If you get in the habit of hitting your child when you're angry, there may come a time when you can't control it.

166. No Biting or Hitting

Toddlers often have trouble expressing their feelings with words, so they tend to do so with their bodies. Here are some ways to help your toddler avoid violent physical behavior.

Encourage empathy. Tell your toddler how other people feel when they're hit or bitten. Toddlers can be quite egocentric, so help him develop an awareness of other people's feelings. Tell him he wouldn't want someone doing that to him, so he shouldn't do it to others.

Say "no!" When your toddler hits another person or animal, tell him firmly, "No hitting!" Explain to him that hitting hurts people. Keep your words simple and clear. If he continues to hurt another, pick him up and take him to another area. If that is not possible, restraint may be needed, but never hurt your child to stop his hitting, kicking, or biting.

Encourage words. Gradually help your toddler use words to express his emotions. Help him learn the names for his feelings (*happy, sad, confused, angry, proud, scared,* and so on). For example, say, "You seem angry. Instead of hitting Johnny, use words to tell him you're angry at him for taking your toy."

Use time-out. Give your child a break to cool off and regain control of his emotions. Take him to another room or another area. (See Tip 172.)

Apology? Most experts believe forcing a toddler to apologize is ineffective, since he's not able to feel remorse yet. Others believe it helps a toddler learn he's done something hurtful and needs to make amends. Either way, encourage your toddler to help the other child feel better.

Monitor situations. Watch out for situations or circumstances that may cause your child to bite or hit someone. Knowing the probable causes may allow you to intercept the behavior and redirect your child's attention.

Use positive reinforcement. If hitting and biting happens frequently, use a sticker chart to keep track of the days when your child is able to avoid hitting or biting. Give him a small reward after a certain number of days, if you like.

Model nonviolence. Never hit or bite your child or anyone else.

167. Quick Tip: Use Your Words

Try to get your child to use his words, even at this early age, instead of biting or hitting. My son was a notorious biter, and I had to watch him carefully. Whenever I thought he might bite another child, I stepped in and encouraged him to say, "I'm angry!" or "I don't like what you did." Then we worked on addressing the situation and resolving any injustices, including those committed by my son.

—Susan W.

168. Whining

Why do toddlers drive us crazy with their whining? They don't mean to. Usually the whining starts when their needs are not met. Here are some tips to minimize whining.

Your toddler wants attention. In most cases, your child isn't getting the attention he wants, so he repeats himself and stretches out his words in a nasally, singsong manner. As his whining goes on and on, he may gradually forget what his initial plea was. Listen and respond to your child when he speaks normally, and he probably won't have to whine.

Your toddler isn't feeling well. Sometimes he whines because he's tired, bored, hungry, upset, or excited or because he's coming down with a cold or other illness. This often leads to crying if he's not attended to. See if you can find the root of the problem and look for a solution. He may need a nap, some cuddling, or perhaps a checkup with the doctor.

Your toddler can't express himself. If you toddler has trouble expressing his feelings or telling you what he wants, he may whine rather than articulate his needs clearly. If you're too attentive to his whining, he doesn't have to talk—therefore, you reinforce the behavior. Ask him to use his words, even one or two, to lessen the whining. If your child can't express himself with words, try to express the words for him.

Praise him. If you have a constant whiner, praise him when he speaks normally. Tell him you can understand him better and that you like his grown-up voice. Then respond to his needs. Don't punish him or yell at him for whining, and never label him a "whiner"—that just reinforces the negative behavior.

169. Quick Tip: Prevention and Distraction

Prevention and distraction are two techniques that work for me. When my toddler begins whining, I usually distract him, and that solves the problem most of the time. Otherwise I try to avoid situations that cause whining. I anticipate when he's tired or hungry or bored, and I take care of it before it becomes a problem.

—Orlando T.

170. Dealing with Negativity

At some point during the toddler years, your usually happy child may enter a negative stage in which he frequently refuses to cooperate and says "no" to just about everything. This is actually a healthy sign of emerging independence. Here are some tips to cope with this stage.

Minimize saying "no." If you minimize saying "no," you may prevent your toddler from saying it too much. Save "no" for the important issues like safety, hurting people, or the destruction of property.

Respect your toddler's wishes. When your toddler says "no," try to understand the meaning behind it. From time to time, in appropriate circumstances, allow him to say it. Honor his wish, so he feels he has some control over his life.

Offer choices. When possible, give your toddler choices instead of telling him what to do. This will help him feel more independent and give him a sense of control.

Redirect. Distract your toddler with an interesting object or activity to stop him from continuing a negative behavior.

Ignore it. Try to overlook minor negativity if you suspect it's being done just to get your attention. Then, if possible, give your child the attention he needs.

171. Catch Him Being Good

One of the best ways to guide your toddler's behavior is through positive reinforcement. Here are some tips to help you shape your toddler's behavior.

Remark on good behavior. Watch for positive behavior and comment when you see it. For example, you might say, "You're using a nice quiet voice today!" Such a remark increases your child's self-esteem and often leads to more positive behavior. On the other hand, saying, "Stop screaming!" when your toddler is having a fit is less effective in shaping the behavior you want.

Be specific with praise. When your toddler does something good, praise him in specific terms to reinforce the good behavior. For example, if he cleans up a mess, say, "You cleaned up that mess so well!" instead of the more general comment, "You're such a good boy!" Likewise, instead of saying, "You're the best artist on the planet," say, "I love the way you use all that color!" Praise the behavior rather than his person.

Use positive language. When your toddler is misbehaving, encouraging words are much more effective than critical ones. For example, instead of saying, "Stop pounding," say, "Please tap softly."

Praise progress. Talk to your toddler about the progress he's making as he works on new skills. If he has problems or setbacks, comment on his efforts and the improvements he's made. Let him know he'll soon be able to do even more.

172. Use Time-Outs

When your toddler is behaving inappropriately and won't stop, remove him from the situation so he can redirect his energy. Use the "time-out" as a respite for your toddler, not as a punishment. A time-out gives your child an opportunity to calm down, think about his behavior, and rejoin the situation with a different perspective.

Give your child a break. Be clear that the point of a time-out is to give your toddler a break, not to punish him. It's a positive way of allowing your toddler to separate himself from a problem and regroup.

Use an appropriate time limit. Most parents use one minute for each year of age. For example, a two-year-old should have a time-out no longer than two minutes. If your child needs more time to calm down, extend it for a minute or two. If the situation seems resolved after a shorter period of time, let your toddler out early. Some parents let their toddler decide when he's ready to rejoin the play. Decide for yourself what works best for your child.

Use time-outs sparingly. As with saying "no," limit your use of time-outs so they remain effective when you need them. Use a time-out only when you think your toddler needs a break from a situation or needs to calm down. Don't use a time-out for every minor problem that comes up, or it will quickly lose its impact.

Talk about it. As your toddler begins his time-out, offer him an explanation of why he's there and what he might want to think about.

Check in. When the time-out has elapsed, talk to your toddler about the problem so he can learn to avoid it in the future. Be supportive and encouraging rather than negative and critical.

Take a turn yourself. If you feel frustration beginning to boil over, give yourself a few minutes to calm down and regroup. Make sure your child is safe, and then step aside and spend a few minutes calming down.

Chapter 8
Playing and Learning

173. How Play Develops

During the toddler years, your child's primary task is to play. This is the way she learns about her world and develops her cognitive skills, fine motor skills, gross motor skills, social skills, emotional awareness, and self-esteem. Here's a look at the different stages of play and how you can encourage your child's development.

Onlooker play. Around age one, your child observes other children at play. Even though she may not engage in the play physically, she participates mentally and learns by watching the other children. Give her plenty of opportunities to watch other kids play.

Solitary play. From ages one to two years, your toddler actively engages in solitary play—pounding, throwing, punching buttons, exploring properties of toys, and so on. She plays by herself, even though there may be other children around, because she's unaware of what other children are doing. Give her plenty of room to enjoy solitary play, but also encourage the development of social play by putting her in situations where she's around other children.

Parallel play. From ages two to three years, your toddler enjoys playing side by side with other children. They may play with the same toys, but they don't interact much at this stage. If you watch your child closely, you'll see she's playing in a similar way with other children, but there's little or no communication or collaboration. Nevertheless, there's a sense of playing "together," so invite a friend the same age over to play with your toddler.

Associative play. From ages three to four, your child communicates, shares materials, and plays the same game or activity with other children. But if you look closely, she's still playing somewhat separately from the other children, even though they're interacting and sharing toys. Offer them activities they can play together to help facilitate their emerging sense of cooperation.

Cooperative play. From ages four to five, your child learns how to play with other children, take on different roles, create an imaginary scene, or take turns at a game. Children begin to share the same goal during play and work together to accomplish it.

174. Play Dates

Play dates offer a valuable natural forum for your toddler to develop many skills, especially language and social skills. Here are guidelines for getting the most out of play dates.

Invite only one. Start out slowly with just one other parent and toddler. Allow your child to become used to playing with (or along side) another child. Later, you may want to expand the group, but four toddlers are about the limit for a successful play date.

Time it right. Set a time, such as midmorning, when the toddlers are at their best. Overtired, hungry, or cranky kids won't add to the fun. And avoid overscheduling. Every day or even every other day is probably too often; once or twice a week is about right.

Start in neutral territory. Schedule the first few play dates on neutral ground, such as at a park with playground equipment or at an indoor community play area. That way neither child will have the advantage with "well, it's *my* house" behavior. Pack up a few toys, some snacks, and the sunscreen if you'll be outside.

Prepare ahead of time. For play dates in the home, minimize your toddler's stress by letting her pick out a few of her favorite toys she doesn't want to share, and stow them away. Set out toys you have more than one of, such as dolls, stuffed animals, books, and blocks. You may want to find some inexpensive toys and buy two or more of each—for example, two red trucks, two dolls, two bottles of bubbles.

Keep expectations realistic. Toddlers don't know how to share—they have to learn and it will take time. Be ready for the inevitable tug-of-war over some of the toys. Try to let the toddlers work it out themselves, but intervene if hitting or scratching begins.

Have diversions waiting in the wings. If fighting or negativity continues too long, change pace with some music and coloring or Play-Doh, or serve a healthy snack such as juice, cheese cubes, and apple slices.

Praise positive behavior. If either child manages to share a toy or wait for her turn, congratulate her. For example, say, "That was nice that you let Jasmine play with your bear. That made her really happy!"

Supervise closely. You and the other parent will probably enjoy exchanging toddler stories and comparing notes on parenting, but watch your toddlers at all times and be ready to participate, assist, or intervene whenever needed.

175. Quick Tip:
Play Date Strategy

Keep your toddler's play dates with other children short, so the kids don't burn out and break down. Kids tend to become overwhelmed easily at this age!

—Dana M.

176. Stimulating Imagination and Creativity

Your toddler begins to use her imagination as early as 18 months. She'll play more and more make-believe as her creativity increases. Here are some tips for sparking that budding imagination.

Open-ended toys. Give your toddler open-ended toys that can be played with in more than one way. For example, a ball can be played with in a number of ways—rolling, kicking, bouncing, throwing—while a wind-up train only goes forward. (See Tip 190.)

Household objects. Offer your toddler objects from around the house and see what she does with them. Give her a cardboard box, a plastic bowl and wooden spoon, a scarf, a sheet of paper, a ribbon, a hat, or another object she can play with creatively. (See Tip 191.)

Arts and crafts. Provide arts and crafts materials to help your toddler express her creativity. (See Tip 225.)

Imagination box. Each evening, put a surprise object (a feather, a clothespin, a rubber band, and so on) in a box and close it. In the morning, have your toddler open it. Then ask her to come up with three things she could do with the object.

Read adventure stories. Let your toddler imagine the action and make the adventure come to life in her mind. Then ask questions to stimulate her imagination further. For example, "Let's make up a different ending. What else could have happened to Jimmy?" or "Now, could you tell me a little story about a dog?"

177. Quick Tip: Limit Gifts

I think children should learn to play without relying on a lot of possessions. It's a good idea to limit gifts at birthdays and holidays. Children learn to be much more creative if they don't have a lot of junk lying around.

—Anne G.

178. Quick Tip: Amazing Box

My toddler got all kinds of nice gifts for his birthday, but the one thing he loved the most was a big box that held one of the gifts! He spent more time sitting in that box—making car noises, pretending to drive around, turning it upside down and hiding inside—than he spent playing with the toy it housed. From then on, we always saved our big boxes for him to play with.

—Shanice A.

179. Sensory-Motor Play

Your toddler develops physically, cognitively, emotionally, psychologically, and socially through different types of play. One way your toddler learns is through sensory-motor play in which she uses her five senses (sight, smell, taste, hearing, and touch) and her fine motor and gross motor skills. Here are some tips for enhancing sensory-motor play.

Water play. Let your toddler play in the bathtub, kiddy pool, kitchen sink, or other large tub filled with water (under your supervision, of course). Provide lots of sink and float toys, plastic cups, water paints, and other tub toys. (See Tip 45.) Color the water with food coloring or add bubble bath. If she's outdoors, turn on the hose and let her experiment with the sprayer.

Sand play. Fill a large plastic tub, sandbox, or kiddy pool with sand, and let your toddler explore it using her senses and motor skills. Give her small toys for imaginary play, such as pails, sifters, shovels, rakes, plastic and paper cups, little plastic figures, cars, and trucks. Add water to part of the sand and let her discover the changed properties of the sand. Help her build hills and castlelike structures with the wet sand. Encourage her to dig, pour, sift, and bury things in the sand. Make sure to cover the sandbox when it's not in use to prevent animals from using it.

Clay play. Give your toddler a handful of clay to explore with her senses. Clay and Play-Doh have different properties, so let her compare them and use them in similar and different ways. Provide tools such as cookie cutters, plastic knives, a garlic press, Popsicle sticks, and other manipulatives. Bake her creation and let your child paint it when it's cool.

Outside play. Take your toddler outside and let her explore the grass, trees, and other natural objects. Have her roll on the lawn, do somersaults, crawl, run, find clover, and pull up handfuls of grass. When it rains, take her outside to listen to, feel, and even taste it. Take a nature walk and help her explore different plants and animals, small hills, rocky areas, or whatever else you come upon. Stand still and listen for birds; feel the breezy air and the heat from the sun. Be careful not to let her near poison ivy or other dangerous vegetation.

180. Mastery Play

As your toddler's play progresses, her fine and gross motor skills develop rapidly. She enjoys doing a task over and over, practicing it to perfection. She may get frustrated easily, so help her if she gets stuck. But try not to interfere too much, so she can learn to solve her own problems.

Climbing. Help your toddler practice climbing up and down steps. This may be a little tricky for her in the beginning. Encourage her to hold on to railings, if possible. Also let her have a chance to explore stepstools, small ladders, and outdoor climbing structures.

Puzzles and other manipulatives. Buy or make simple puzzles containing only a few pieces to get your toddler started. Provide more challenging puzzles as her skills develop. You might also offer her Duplos, pegboards, light-up boards, and so on.

Nesting and stacking. Give your toddler bowls, cups, and blocks that nest or stack. These will help her learn to put objects in a series and to understand size, spatial relationships, and balance. They'll also enhance her eye-hand coordination and fine-tune her hand and finger movements.

181. Rough-and-Tumble Play

Essentially, rough-and-tumble play is safe roughhousing in which a child sometimes uses a play face that looks intense and even angry at times. Rough-and-tumble play is more common among boys than girls, but girls enjoy it, too. Keep an eye on your child and any others, so they don't get carried away and hurt each other.

Wrestling. Get down on the floor and wrestle with your toddler, gently flipping her over and pinning her down briefly. Let her pin you, too, so she doesn't feel overwhelmed and overpowered.

Somersaults. Let your toddler practice somersaults on the lawn or carpet (or on a mat or folded blanket on a hardwood floor).

Chase. Let your toddler chase you around the yard, or have her chase after a ball or other moving toy.

Red light, green light. Have your toddler run across the yard when you say "green light," and have her stop when you say "red light." Pause for different lengths of time before calling "red light" and see how far she makes it each time.

Tiger tail. Stick a piece of fabric or a paper towel into the back of your toddler's waistband, and do the same with yours. Then have her run around and try to grab the tiger tail from your pants while preventing you from grabbing hers.

182. Animal Fun

As your toddler becomes more skilled in her gross motor movements, play games to challenge her motor skills, cognitive development, and social interaction. Here are some ideas for animal games.

Moo and peep. Show your toddler pictures of animals, and make the animal's sound as you look at each picture. Have your toddler imitate you. Then get out a tape recorder and record your toddler making the noises. Play the tape back and have your toddler identify what animal goes with each sound.

Walk like an animal. Find pictures of animals that have distinct "walks"—such as an elephant, frog, snake, rabbit, and duck—and show them to your toddler. Select a picture and have your child walk as that animal would. (Show her how if she doesn't know.) Put on some marching music for added fun.

Create a critter. Cut out pictures of animals and show them to your toddler. Cut off various body parts (heads, arms, legs, tails) and arrange them in front of her. Have your toddler put together a new critter using any of the body parts, and glue the new beast onto a large sheet of paper. Together, you might want to make up a story to go with the critter.

183. Dramatic Play

Toddlers have vivid imaginations that emerge in dramatic play. Your toddler uses her imagination to create scenes in which she acts out different roles from different stories. She might make up her own stories or borrow plot elements from books she's read or videos she's seen. Such creativity is important to your child's development.

House. Playing "house" is one of the most popular forms of dramatic play by young children, perhaps because the situations are familiar and props are handy. Your toddler can assume the roles of mother, father, sibling, baby, pet, or any other relative.

Boxes. Use a large cardboard box to help your child build a house, spaceship, or store. Cut windows in the sides, make an opening for a doorway, and so on. Decorate the inside and outside to make it seem authentic.

Sheets. Drape sheets or blankets over tables or furniture to make a house, fort, hideout, or other structure. For example, your child might pretend the draped place is a spaceship or a castle.

Accessories. Provide accessories such as plastic dishes, toy food, small cardboard boxes, and dress-up clothes.

Stories. Read stories, fairy tales, and folktales to your toddler to stimulate her imagination.

184. Playing Doctor

Another popular type of dramatic play among young children is the imaginative reenactment of doctor visits, illnesses, hospital emergencies, or other medical situations. This type of play helps your toddler act out circumstances that may be frightening or difficult for her to understand or control. Your toddler may assume the role of the doctor or nurse, the sick or dying person, or even the ambulance driver. Sometimes she may switch roles as she plays.

Hospital. Set up a hospital or doctor's office to help set the scene. Use a small table for the reception desk, some books and magazines for the waiting room, and cushions on the floor for the examination table.

Props. Provide props such as toy stethoscopes, syringes, blood pressure devices, and Band-Aids.

Patients. Provide patients in the form of dolls or stuffed animals (or yourself) if your toddler wants to be the doctor. That way she can administer aid and comfort to one or more patients.

185. Playing Monster

Another common form of dramatic play is monster play in which a child gets involved with a scary monster or "bad guy." Usually the child is being chased or otherwise threatened by the monster. This type of play can be somewhat aggressive at times, but there's usually no need to be concerned. Your toddler is merely acting out her fears and dealing with them in a safe, healthy way. But be prepared—she's apt to do lots of growling, yelling, and screaming during monster play!

Hero. If your toddler wants to play the role of the hero who defeats a monster, she'll probably need some special powers. Bestow magical powers on her so she can save the day. Her special power might be lightening bolts, water blasts, the ability to make things disappear, and so on. Let her dress up in a store-bought superhero costume, or make a cape or wings by pinning a towel or scarf to the back of her shirt.

Victim. If your toddler wants to play the role of the victim, designate a place where she can hide from the monster. You might also create a jail-like area where the monster keeps her captured until she escapes.

Monster. Sometimes your toddler will want to play the role of the monster. This makes her feel powerful and in control of the other characters. Besides, it's just plain fun to be the scary monster sometimes!

186. Hide-and-Seek

As a toddler, your toddler understands object permanence, which means she understands that things still exist even though she can't see them. It also means she's ready to play hide-and-seek—and variations of it.

Where's the toy? Choose a favorite toy and show it to your toddler. Tell her to close her eyes while you hide the toy somewhere in the room (in plain view). Have her open her eyes and look for the toy. Give her clues to help her find it if she needs assistance. Take turns hiding and looking for toys.

I hear something. Have your toddler close her eyes. Then turn on a musical toy as you hide it under a pillow, blanket, or some other object in the room. Have your toddler open her eyes and try to find the toy by searching for the sound.

Where's Mommy/Daddy? Have your toddler close her eyes while you hide somewhere in the room. Then let her try to find you. Make some noises if she needs help. Expand the game to more rooms if she's ready for that.

Treasure hunt. Hide four or five special toys or other items around the room. Tell your toddler what they are, give her a basket, and have her try to find them. Then let her hide some toys for you to find.

187. Sorting Games

Your older toddler's cognitive skills develop rapidly, so have her play fun games that increase her thinking and classification skills.

Muffin mix-up. Get out a muffin pan, bowl, and several kinds of cereals. Put a small handful of each cereal into the bowl and mix them up. Have your toddler sort the cereals into the muffin pan cups.

Color coordinated. Get out a variety of solid-colored items. You might use toys, plastic items, crayons, and so on. Have your toddler group them according to color.

Go together. Pick out objects that clearly go together, such as a shoe and sock, a plate and cup, a washcloth and soap, a book and bookmark, and so on. Mix up the objects on the floor and have your toddler try to match them. Talk about why they match.

Laundry pile. While you're sorting clean laundry, have your toddler pick out the clothes that belong to her. Have her try to sort the other clothes according to their owners. Give her some clues if she needs help.

188. Fun with the Senses

Children learn about their world through their senses. Here are some ideas for enjoying sensory play.

Smell, taste, and feel. Set out three bowls and place a different aromatic food in each bowl, such as strawberry jam, a chocolate brownie, and freshly cut orange slices. Have your toddler close her eyes, then have her smell, taste, and feel each food. See if she can guess what each is.

See and say. Set out three objects that are similar but different, such as three trucks in different sizes and colors. Have your child tell you how they're similar and how they're different.

Touch and tell. Place some familiar items in an opaque plastic bag. Have your toddler reach inside, feel the objects, then try to guess what each is. While she is touching them, ask her to tell you how they feel (soft, fuzzy, cold, and so on). Give her some clues if she's having trouble.

189. Developmental Tasks

When providing toys for your toddler, think about what she'll be learning when she plays with them. Here are some basic tasks your toddler can practice while playing.

- Filling containers with objects, such as putting rocks in a bucket or jellybeans in a jar.
- Pouring the contents of a container or transferring the contents from one container into another, such as pouring water from a cup to a bowl.
- Stacking two or more objects, such as blocks, on top of each other.
- Nesting objects inside one another according to size, such as putting a medium bowl inside a large bowl and then putting a small bowl inside the medium bowl.
- Sorting objects in different groups according to shared qualities, such as dividing up different beans by color, size, or shape.
- Measuring a certain amount of something into a container, such as measuring ½ cup of cereal.
- Sequencing objects in order according to size, such as lining up toys from small to large.
- Comparing and contrasting two objects, such as two different tricycles, and noticing how they are similar and how they are different.

- Drumming various objects on various surfaces, such as banging a wooden spoon on the bottom of a pan or bucket.

190. Best Toys: The Basics

Here are some popular toys that give your toddler opportunities to develop important skills.

Shakers and rattles. Your toddler enjoys the sounds and vibrations of noise-making toys, and she learns about cause and effect when she plays with them.

Push toys, pull toys. Your toddler practices her gross motor skills and problem-solving skills as she pulls or pushes toys around the room.

Blocks. Your toddler learns spatial relationships, cognitive skills, problem solving, and creative thinking while she plays with blocks.

Puzzles. Your toddler learns spatial relationships and problem-solving skills as she learns to put simple puzzles together.

Bubbles. Your toddler develops eye-hand coordination and fine motor control as she blows, catches, and pops bubbles.

Play-Doh. Your toddler enjoys exploring the tactile properties of Play-Doh, and she uses her imagination, creativity, and fine motor skills as she squeezes, pounds, rolls, and manipulates the Play-Doh.

Finger paints. Your toddler experiences the sensory enjoyment of moving her hands around in finger paints (or pudding), and she learns fine motor skills, expresses her emotions, and feels proud of her accomplishment.

Shape box. Your toddler learns geometric shapes by sorting them in a shape box. Understanding these basic concepts leads to higher levels of cognitive development, sorting, and classification.

Ball. Your toddler enhances her eye-hand coordination, fine and gross motor skills, and spatial relationships as she learns to roll, catch, throw, and kick a ball.

191. Best Toys: Household Objects

Toddlers enjoy toys that appeal to their senses. Here are some suggestions for household toys that will enhance her physical, cognitive, and psychological development.

- Aluminum pie tins
- Balled-up socks
- Baster
- Cardboard tubes
- Empty boxes
- Lids
- Measuring cups
- Pan and wooden spoon
- Plastic bottles
- Plastic bowls
- Plastic cookie cutters
- Plastic cups
- Plastic plates and silverware
- Sponge
- Table covered with blanket or sheet
- Tongs

192. Best Toys: Puppets

As your toddler begins to acquire language, she begins to enjoy doll and puppet play. Using puppets with your toddler is a great way to enhance her vocabulary, stimulate her imagination, help her express her feelings, and help her develop social skills. Here are some tips for puppet play with your toddler.

Paper-bag puppets. Let your toddler decorate two lunch bags using yarn or cotton for hair and cut-out paper shapes for eyes, nose, mouth, and ears. Help her slip on the paper-bag puppets and act out a story. Your child may want to play both puppets, or she may want to give one puppet to you so you can act out a story together.

Wooden-spoon puppets. Using permanent markers, draw faces on a couple of large wooden spoons or tongue depressors (available at pharmacies). Wrap a piece of fabric around the handle just below the spoon, and tape it on so the fabric "gown" will hide your toddler's hand when she holds the spoon. Then have fun making your wooden puppets dance and talk.

Garden-glove puppets. Find a pair of small, plain muslin garden gloves—one glove for each of you. Pick a theme such as "five little monkeys" or "five little piggies." Use fine-point permanent markers to decorate the finger-tips with funny faces, or attach small felt pieces and pom-poms with a glue stick. Slip on the gloves and sing finger plays (songs with accompanying body movements) that match the characters. (See Tips 274 and 275.)

Personalized paper-doll puppet. Treat your toddler to a special puppet that looks just like her! Cut out a paper-doll shape from poster board. Find a close-up photo of your toddler (one you don't mind using), cut her head out, and glue it over the paper doll's head. Add clothing details with crayons or a permanent marker (or make several outfits from paper), and let your toddler play with her cute paper-doll puppet.

Sock puppets. Use a permanent marker to turn large white socks into animals or funny characters. Then slip the sock puppets on your hands and share a funny conversation with your toddler.

193. Quick Tip: Puppet Play

My son loves to make puppets out of socks and paper bags. He saves most of them, so now he has quite a collection—including boys, girls, moms, dads, clowns, animals, and even monsters. When he wants to play puppets, I read an action story, and he acts out the story with his choice of puppets.

–Jake B.

194. Quick Tip: Finger Friends

I use a nontoxic marker to draw faces with different expressions on the tips of my toddler's fingers. (Sometimes we use a glove.) My toddler likes to name each of the faces. Then he makes up a story, acting it out with his new finger friends.
—Jonathan P.

195. Best Toys: Dress-Up Play

To help your toddler develop her imagination, let her dress up in different clothes or costumes and act out different roles. Here are some suggestions for your toddler's dress-up box.

- Dresses
- Skirts
- Blouses and shirts
- Pants and shorts
- Jackets and coats
- Ties
- Shoes
- Socks
- Hats
- Jewelry and watches
- Vests
- Aprons and smocks
- Purses
- Scarves
- Capes
- Backpacks
- Gloves and mittens
- Plastic "glasses" and sunglasses
- Fake mustache
- Fake beard
- Play tiara
- Play crown

196. Quick Tip: Silly Dress-Up Fun

I stopped by a thrift shop occasionally, and I picked up a few clothes for my toddler's dress-up play. I got a funny pair of slippers, a sequined vest, a long scarf with fringe, white gloves, a polka-dot dress, a silly hat, and some costume jewelry. I spread out the clothes on my daughter's bed and let her dress up in the outfit of her choice. She played for hours in her crazy creation, and gradually we've added more items to her very important dress-up box.

—Cheryl W.

197. Best Toys: Safe Toys

Periodically, make sure your toddler's toys and playthings are safe so she doesn't get hurt while playing.

- No sharp edges or points
- No rough surfaces
- No small pieces that can break off
- No small parts that can be swallowed
- No glitter, Styrofoam, or plastic bags
- Safe if put in your toddler's mouth
- No long strings or cords that can get wrapped around your child's neck
- No moving parts that could pinch your child's skin
- Age-appropriate
- Clean
- Germfree

198. Quick Tip: Best Plaything

The very best plaything for your toddler is YOU. Spend time with him, talk, listen, sing, dance, do arts and crafts, dress up, play games, read, act silly, and enjoy your time together. You're more fun for him than anything else.

—Maria L.

Chapter 9
Outdoor Play and Safety

199. Outdoor Play

Playing outdoors helps your toddler learn to control his arms, legs, and body, and it helps him develop his balance and coordination. The great outdoors offers all kinds of opportunities for learning.

Balls. Give your toddler lots of balls to bounce, throw, and catch. Offer him a variety of balls including beach balls, rubber balls, plastic balls, tennis balls, and whiffleballs. Teach your toddler how to throw a ball into a bucket, knock over a lightweight toy with the ball, roll the ball uphill and watch it come back, sit on a ball and bounce, and other activities and games.

Water play. Fill a kiddy pool with water and let your toddler splash and soak. Give him water toys to enjoy in the pool, such as plastic boats, squirters, cups, watering cans, and so on. Make sure to watch your toddler at all times around water. (See Tip 210.)

Push toys, pull toys. Give your toddler a wagon to pull, and encourage him to load it with toys to transport around the yard. Give him a toy lawnmower or wheelbarrow to push so he can pretend to cut the grass or carry more toys.

World of wheels. Let your child pedal his way around the yard, sidewalk, or driveway on a Big Wheel or small tricycle. Make sure he wears a helmet, and remind him of safety rules so he doesn't get hurt.

Sandbox. Fill a kiddy pool or sandbox with sand and let your toddler play and explore the properties of sand. (See Tip 179.)

200. Out and About: A Whole New World

Here are a few other outdoor items and areas that can provide fun and helpful gross motor challenges for your toddler.

- Booster swings
- Hose and sprinkler
- Large area for running
- Lawn for rolling and somersaults
- Nature trails for walking and learning
- Playground swings, slides, merry-go-round, and climbing structures
- Small hill to climb

201. Fun in the Great Outdoors

Here are some activities for having fun outdoors with your toddler.

Make chalk pictures. Give your toddler large pieces of chalk and let him decorate the driveway or sidewalk. Draw his shadow and turn it into a superhero with colorful details. Create a path for his tricycle to follow, make squares to step in, draw funny faces of family members, and so on.

Enjoy a treasure hunt. Hide some toys in the yard and have your toddler try to find them. (Don't make it too tough, though.) Let him take a turn hiding toys for you to find. Go on a treasure hunt for pine cones, rocks, and so on.

Play follow-the-leader. Tell your toddler to follow you as you move around the yard or park. Use different types of walks, duck under obstacles, climb a small hill, flap your arms like a bird, and be generally creative and fun loving. Let your toddler have a turn being the leader, too.

Make a collage. Have your toddler collect leaves, flowers, dandelions, pine cones, pine needles, small sticks, pebbles, and other objects from the yard. Lay them out on a large sheet of paper and let him glue them on in a creative design. Talk about the collage, and together write a short story to go with it.

Take a walk. Explore your neighborhood, a nearby park, or a downtown area with your toddler. Let him be the guide, if possible, and talk about what you see, hear, and smell along the way.

202. Quick Tip: Random Walk

Whenever my toddler and I took walks around the neighborhood, I'd start the walk by asking him, "Which way do you want to go?" He'd point in the direction he wanted to take, and off we went. Each time we reached a corner, he'd get to choose the direction. He loved being in control and making choices. At the same time it taught him concepts such as left, right, and straight. We had lots of fun and got to see many different parts of our neighborhood.

—Ann P.

203. Quick Tip: Happy Trails

When I go out with my toddler, whether it's just for a walk or a trip, I always bring extra clothes and underwear for him. You never know what will happen with a three-year-old. I also bring along something to play with in case there's a lull in an activity, a snack in case he gets hungry or cranky, and my cell phone in case of emergency.

—Dana M.

204. Outdoor Safety

Although there's lots of fun stuff to discover outdoors, there are definite dangers as well. Here are some tips for keeping your toddler safe.

- Never leave your toddler unattended while he's outside.
- Cover your toddler's exposed skin with sunscreen before you go outside. (See Tip 207.)
- Check outdoor toys and equipment to make sure they're safe (no sharp edges, broken parts, or hot spots).
- Provide a soft area for your toddler to play on, if possible. If he takes a tumble, he'll be less likely to hurt himself.
- Watch out for stray animals when you're walking or playing outside, since they can be unpredictable.
- If your toddler is playing with or near other children, keep an eye on them to make sure they're not playing too rough, throwing sand, or doing something that might hurt someone.
- Put your toddler in a stroller if you want to keep him extra safe when you're out and about.

205. Quick Tip: Stroller Rules

To make sure my girls are safe when we're walking outside, I keep them in the stroller. If they get squirmy and want out, I have them walk holding onto the stroller. If they let go, they have to get back in the stroller.
—Dana M.

206. Quick Tip: Stroller Rollover

I learned two lessons about the stroller the hard way. The first time was when I loaded up the handles with packages and my purse. It became so top-heavy it tipped over—with my toddler still in the seat! The second time I forgot to use the brake, and my toddler started rolling down a small hill! It's one thing to buy a stroller that's safe, but it's another to make sure you use it safely!
—Lin L.

207. Too Much Sun

Your toddler loves to play outside on sunny days, but you need to be especially diligent about preventing over-exposure to the sun. Young children burn easily in the sun, since they haven't been exposed much in their early years. Here are some tips to keep in mind.

Apply sunscreen. Apply sunscreen with a sun protection factor (SPF) of 15 or higher every time your toddler heads outside, even on cloudy days.

Avoid direct sunlight. Try to stay out of direct sunlight during the peak hours from 10:00 A.M. to 2:00 P.M., and avoid too many hours in the sun without a break in the shade or indoors.

Keep him cool and refreshed. Keep your toddler covered with loose cotton clothing. Give him sunglasses and a hat to wear in the sun. Refresh him with lots of liquids throughout the day.

Treat sunburn. If your toddler does get a sunburn, give him plenty of cool water or other drinks to rehydrate him. Put him in a tepid bath and offer an age-appropriate dose of ibuprofen for any swelling or pain. Call your doctor if your toddler shows signs of heat stroke—lethargy, crying, confusion, loss of consciousness, and a fever of 104°F or higher.

208. Stinging Insects

Bugs fascinate toddlers, but you don't want bees (or wasps or hornets) bugging him while he's outside playing. Keep these tips in mind.

Don't attract. Pay special attention to garbage cans, gardens in bloom, and food that's been left out, since the smells attract bees. Avoid dressing your toddler in bright colors, which also attract bees, when he's going outside to play.

Treat a sting. If your toddler is stung, look for a reddened area on exposed parts of his body. Scrape out the stinger with the back of your fingernail, being careful not to push it in farther. Rub the area with ice to curb the pain and swelling. Or soothe the pain after you've removed the stinger by spreading a thick paste made from a little baking soda and water on the affected area.

Watch for reaction. If your toddler has any breathing difficulties, call 911. Keep a bee sting kit handy in case of allergic reaction.

209. Hazards in Your Own Yard

Here are tips to keep your toddler safe in outdoor areas around your home.

Driveway. Car accidents are the leading cause of death among children. Some accidents occur before the car even leaves the driveway. Lock your car when it's not in use, and make sure it's parked safely. Always store the car keys out of your child's reach—even a three-year-old has been known to  drive a car! Teach your toddler not to play in or near the car. Always walk behind your car before you back it up to make sure all is clear. Be extremely careful when backing up a car in the driveway, especially if you're driving a large SUV or truck. If you do let your toddler play in the driveway, make sure he's protected from running into the street. Never leave your toddler in a parked car.

Barbecue. In the United States, nearly five thousand children are treated for barbecue burns each year. The best way to prevent injuries is to keep your toddler away from the grill. Don't let him play near the barbecue or stand too close to it. Even if you've finished grilling, the barbecue stays hot for some time, so keep your eye on your toddler at all times. If your toddler touches the hot metal, run the affected area under cold water. If a blister appears, the burn may be serious, so check with your doctor. Store lighter fluid, matches, charcoal, electric starters, and cooking utensils out of your toddler's reach. Keep a fire extinguisher nearby. Lock your barbecue away when not in use.

Gardening tools. While you're gardening or doing yardwork, keep an extra eye on your toddler. Make sure your lawnmower is not accessible to him. Never let him ride on the lawnmower with you. Lock up all lawn and garden tools. Also lock up fertilizers, pesticides, and weed killers, or be sure they are out of your toddler's reach. When you're working in the yard or garden, you might want give your toddler some toy gardening tools to play with so he's less interested in your tools and materials.

Poisonous plants. Some toddlers will eat anything that appeals to them, including pretty flowers and plants. Teach your toddler not to eat anything outdoors without permission. Any plant is potentially dangerous if a child tries to eat it and chokes on it. Call poison control to find out which plants are poisonous in your yard, and always have the poison control number handy.

210. Swimming Pool Safety

Swimming pools are one of the leading causes of death for young children. They may be entranced by the water and not aware of how dangerous falling in could be. Here are some important pool safety tips.

Kiddy pools. Young children can drown in 1 inch of water, so even the kiddy pool can be dangerous if your toddler is unattended. Most pool accidents occur when a toddler wanders outside unexpectedly. Make sure your child learns to walk and not run around the kiddy pool as he could easily slip and fall into the water. When you're finished using the kiddy pool, empty it.

Gates. Most states require that larger swimming pools be gated. Make sure the gates are locked at all times. They should close and latch automatically, and the latch should be higher than your toddler's reach. The surrounding fence should be at least 5 feet tall.

Sitters. Remind caregivers, sitters, and relatives about pool safety, since they may not be as aware of the dangers as you are. Double-check to make sure pool gates are locked before you leave your toddler in the care of others.

Locks. Install locks on all doors and windows that lead to the pool area, and make sure your toddler can't get to the pool without your knowledge.

Watch. Never leave your toddler unattended by a swimming pool—*never*. Don't leave him in the care of other young children either. They can't be relied on to keep your child safe.

Chapter 10
Gross Motor Development

211. Beginning to Walk

Most toddlers learn to walk sometime between 9 and 18 months. Some children are eager to get moving, while others prefer to concentrate on different skills, like fine motor abilities and language development. There's no correlation between when a child learns to walk and her overall physical ability. Once a toddler takes that first step, though, there'll be no stopping her. Give her plenty of encouragement and opportunity to practice, and watch her gross motor skills improve with each step.

Help improve her strength. Help your toddler strengthen her leg muscles to facilitate her transition to walking. Have her push around a cart or other push toy. Encourage her to pull herself up to the couch, hold on, and take a step or two. Hold her in a standing position and let her dance to music.

Hold on. To encourage your toddler to walk, begin by holding her hands while she's standing, then gently lead her a few steps. As she becomes more confident, let her hold your fingers instead of your hands. Eventually she'll be able to walk holding only one of your fingers. Before you know it, she'll let go.

Let her crawl. If your toddler has begun to walk but prefers to crawl, let her. She may be physically ready to walk, but she may lack the confidence. Crawling may feel safer, easier, and more efficient than walking. She'll switch to walking when she's ready.

Don't overdo it. Try not to overdo the practice sessions or insist that your toddler walk. Instead, let her practice when she wants to, and keep it fun.

Set up a cruise area.
Arrange your furniture closer than usual so your toddler has something to hold on to as she's learning to walk. Increase the distance between furniture as she becomes more adept at moving from one piece to another.

212. All Fall Down: Clumsiness

When toddlers first begin walking, they're usually awkward and wobbly. Along the way, your toddler will fall many times and probably pick up a few bumps and bruises. Here are some tips for developing her walking skills while preventing serious injuries.

Watch closely. It's a good idea to stay near your toddler, even if you think she's managing a walking task fairly well, such as climbing up a short ladder at the park. If she slips, you'll be there to catch her.

Let her go. Your toddler likes to be challenged, so little by little let her stretch her abilities, as long as she's safe. You know better than anyone what her tendencies are and how much encouragement and supervision she needs.

Show confidence. Avoid making your child fearful by conveying anxiety at her attempts. Show her you're confident she can accomplish a walking task—but always stay nearby.

Praise. Reward her with praise even when she hasn't completed a walking task. Encouragement will help propel her next time.

Practice. Set aside several times a day when you and your toddler can focus on her walking skills. Walk beside her as she takes a few steps, and offer a hand or finger if she's about to fall. Kneel about six paces in front of her and encourage her to walk to you. With regular practice, your toddler will gradually improve her strength, balance, and coordination. But don't make it drudgery—keep it fun.

213. Watch Me Walk

If possible, avoid putting shoes on your toddler during these first walking months. Walking barefoot will allow her to feel the friction of her foot on the floor, which, in turn, will help her develop her arches, strengthen her ankles, and improve her balance. Here are some other tips for enhancing this important skill.

Clear the space. Move furniture, toys, and other obstacles out of the way so your toddler can toddle around freely. Remove throw rugs or secure them to the floor.

Offer a toy. Offer your toddler a toy to hold in her hand as an extra challenge while walking. Or give her a pull toy to use while walking, and watch her drag it along. You can also set a toy at her feet to encourage her to squat down and pick it up.

Make a path. Lay towels end to end on the carpet and encourage your toddler to walk on the path to improve her balance. Then make a wide curving path for her to follow.

Try new surfaces. Give your toddler the opportunity to walk on different surfaces such as carpet, hardwood floors, linoleum, grass, sand, dirt, concrete, asphalt, and so on.

Give her a challenge. Create a simple obstacle course to challenge her skills. Play follow-the-leader and encourage her to imitate your walking style (regular steps, baby steps, marching, and so on). Have her chase you or a toy you're dragging behind you.

214. Walking Shoes

Your toddler doesn't really need shoes as she's learning to walk, except for warmth if the floor is cold or for protection if she's walking on a rough surface. Most of the time it's best to let her go barefoot. After she's walking fairly well, though, it's time to buy her shoes. Here are some tips to help you find the right ones.

Get the right fit. Have your toddler fitted (while standing) by an experienced salesperson who knows how to measure young children. Both feet should be measured since the right and left foot often differ somewhat in size. The shoes will need to feel comfortable on the larger foot.

Choose flexible shoes. Buy soft leather or canvas shoes that flex with your toddler's feet. You should be able to bend the toe of the shoe up about 40 degrees easily.

Allow wiggle room. Make sure your toddler has enough room to wiggle and curl her toes. There should be a little space above her toes and about ½ inch in front of her toes.

Watch for pressure marks. When you remove the shoes, look for pressure marks on your child's feet. If you find any, avoid those shoes.

Look for good traction. Make sure the shoes have nonskid soles for good traction.

Add comfy socks. Cover your toddler's feet with stretch socks for a comfortable fit. The socks shouldn't be either droopy or tight.

Save your money. Don't spend a lot of money on your toddler's shoes, since she'll probably outgrow them before you get home from the store. Seriously, although buying this first pair is a big event, you'll probably need to buy her second pair in about two or three months.

215. Quick Tip: Shoe Shopping

Now before we go shopping for shoes, I'm always sure my toddler is well rested and has eaten a nutritious meal or snack. The first time he was hot, tired, and hungry—and his cooperation "score" at the shoe store was less than zero. With my new plan, it usually goes much better.

—Quinn D.

216. Quick Tip: Super Shoes

There are some great shoes on the market for toddlers today. In fact, those stiff, heavy, old-fashioned-looking shoes aren't even on the shelves anymore. I bought my son some well-made sneakers with glittery stripes. He loved them.

—Susan W.

217. Big Muscles: Gross Motor Skills

Crawling, cruising, and walking develop your toddler's gross motor skills (movement of arms, legs, and body). She learns to coordinate her large muscles, keep her balance, and move her body through space. All she needs is an opportunity to move and plenty of encouragement from you. Here are some tips for developing her gross motor skills.

Balls. At first, give your toddler large balls to kick, throw, catch, roll, and explore. Then when you think she's ready, start giving her smaller and smaller balls to develop her coordination.

Hammers. Let your toddler pound pegs with a toy hammer set to develop her arm strength and eye-hand coordination.

Playground. Give your toddler time to explore playground equipment at a local park or school so she can develop her climbing skills, grasping skills, coordination, and balance.

Swings. Help your child learn to pump her legs on the swing while she holds on and moves herself back and forth. Start her out with small pushes, and teach her how to bend her legs and rock her body.

Rolling. Have your toddler lie on the grass or carpet with her arms at her sides and have her roll from one side to the other. Then roll her up in a blanket and unroll her.

Dancing. Teach your toddler the "Hokey Pokey" to help her learn what her body parts are, how to move them, how to coordinate them, and how to keep her balance.

Wheels. Let your child ride around on a scooter, tricycle, wagon, or other locomotive toy. Provide a large space for playing with these toys.

219. Dance, Dance, Dance

Toddlers love music. They enjoy swaying their bodies to its rhythm. Dancing improves motor skills, coordination, and balance. All they need is a little music to get them moving and a little guidance to stimulate their actions.

Clap. Begin by having your toddler clap to some music as best as she can.

Sway. Show your toddler how to sway back and forth to the music, moving from one foot to the other.

Jump. Have your toddler jump and hop to the music. Teach her how to change feet while jumping and hopping.

Skip. Show your toddler how to skip around in a circle to the music. This will take time and practice, but she should be able to make some attempts.

Animal dance. Have your toddler choose an animal to imitate. Turn on some music and have her dance the way the animal might dance.

Freeze dance. Turn on some music and have your toddler dance to the beat. After a few seconds stop the music and tell her to "freeze." Then turn on the music again and "unfreeze" her so she can dance again.

Dance till you drop. Turn on some lively music and tell your toddler to dance to the tune. Have her dance until you stop the music, then have her drop to the floor. Have her resume dancing when you start the music again.

"Hokey Pokey." Play or sing the "Hokey Pokey" song and have your toddler move her body parts according to the instructions. Try some other popular songs that encourage your toddler to move her body.

Scarf dance. Give your toddler a long scarf and have her wave it around while moving her body. Play some fun music, and encourage her to make her scarf dance to the beat.

Tag dancing. Turn on some music and have your toddler dance for a few seconds. Then have her tag you so it's your turn to dance. Keep taking turns tagging each other and dancing.

Follow the dancer. Turn on some music and start a simple dance. Have your toddler copy you. Change the dance as you go, and have her copy the new dance. Then let her be the dance leader while you copy her dances.

218. Running and Jumping

Soon after some toddlers learn to walk, they take off running and jumping as fast as they can. Other toddlers take more time and need some help in learning variations on walking.

Different walks. Teach your toddler other ways of getting from place to place. You might want to start with running, galloping, and hopping. Then move on to skipping, leaping, jumping, and so on.

Snatch it! Place some small lightweight items (such as scarves or socks) around the room so they're in plain sight and easily accessible. Tell your toddler to collect the items as fast as she can. After she's finished, put them in different places and let her gather them up again.

Jumping jack. Lay some pieces of paper on the floor, spacing them several feet apart. Have your toddler run around the room and try to jump over each "obstacle." After she runs the course, rearrange them for another jumping session.

Jump and run. Have your toddler make a large circle around you while you call out directions. Tell her to run, jump, hop, roll over, and so on.

Obstacle course. Set up small obstacles for your toddler to run around, such as pillows, soft toys, or small empty boxes. Show your toddler how to run around the obstacles, and then let her try it herself. Change the arrangement of the obstacles each time she runs the course successfully.

220. Let's Play Ball

Playing with a ball helps your toddler improve her gross motor skills, eye-hand coordination, problem-solving skills, and social skills. It also develops her understanding of spatial relationships, cause and effect, and cognitive concepts.

Big ball toss. Get a lightweight plastic or foam ball about 12 inches in diameter and a large basket, tub, or box that will easily hold the ball. Have your toddler stand back a few inches and try to throw the ball into the container. Show her what to do and help her until she gets the hang of it.

Bowling ball. Set up some lightweight containers (such as empty plastic bottles or milk cartons) in a triangular shape on the floor. Give your toddler a large ball, have her stand back a few feet, and tell her to roll the ball toward the containers to knock them over.

Catch it! Sit on the floor opposite your toddler, placing her back against a wall (to stop the ball if she doesn't catch it). Have her open her legs wide while you do the same. Roll and catch a large ball back and forth between your legs.

Tummy time. Have your toddler lay her tummy on top of an extra large ball. Hold onto her waist and roll her around on the ball. Then roll her side to side and back and forth.

222. Gross Motor Play

To further increase your toddler's gross motor skills, think up games that involve her arms, legs, and body, and that improve her coordination and balance.

Run. Have your toddler run as fast as she can from one end of the yard to the other. Time her and see if she can beat her best time. Have her turn corners and stop when you yell the signal.

Jump. Set up about six small obstacles, such as small pillows or stuffed animals, and have your toddler jump over them.

Hop. Have your toddler hop around the yard on two legs, then have her try it on one leg.

Leap. Lay out some wooden planks or other large flat objects, and have your toddler leap from one to the next. Make sure the objects are safe.

Climb. Find safe objects for your toddler to climb up and down. Spot her so she doesn't fall and hurt herself.

One-leg stand. Have your toddler stand on one leg as long as she can, then the other. Have her close her eyes and do the same.

Somersault. Show your toddler how to tuck herself into a ball and roll forward, completing a somersault.

Hopscotch. Mark out a hopscotch course on the sidewalk, driveway, or basement floor. Show your toddler how to hop, leap, and jump from one end to the other.

Lift. Have your toddler try to lift herself up while hanging from a bar. Spot her in case she slips.

221. Developing Motor Skills

At age three, your toddler will make tremendous strides in her gross motor skills. Give her opportunities to exercise these skills and fine-tune her abilities.

Shopping. Let your toddler reach for lightweight items on lower shelves and put them in the cart. She can also push the cart occasionally.

Sweeping the floor. Give your toddler a dustpan and a short broom or sweeping brush, and let her sweep the floor, patio, or sidewalk. Teach her how to fill the dustpan and dump it into the trashcan.

Making the bed. As you spread out the clean sheets, have your toddler help smooth out the wrinkles and tuck in the sheets. Let her put the pillows in the cases, too.

Washing the car. Show your toddler how to spray the car with the hose, scrub the lower parts with a soapy sponge, hose off the soap, and dry the car with old towels.

Chapter 11
Fine Motor Development

223. Drawing Skills

The development of your toddler's fine motor skills (movement of hands, fingers, and toes) correlates with his ability to draw specific types of pictures. Here are the drawing skills your toddler will exhibit at various stages of development and how you can enhance them.

Marks on paper. These are the first signs of control your toddler will exhibit. He may not always watch what he's doing, but he's aware that he's "drawing."

To help: Provide large sheets of white paper and large crayons or washable markers that are easy to hold. Put newspaper down under the paper if he's having trouble staying within its boundaries, and encourage him to make marks on the paper only. Give him lots of praise for his efforts.

Abstract designs. Next your toddler makes abstract (nonpictorial) designs. He moves the marker across the paper continuously. (He can't yet stop, lift the marker, move it, and start again, which takes more coordination and skill.)

To help: Gently guide your toddler's hand over the paper to give him the feeling of continuous movement. Once he gets the hang of it, let go and let him do it himself.

Simple shapes. At this stage your toddler draws simple shapes (circles, squares, and triangles) with clear starting and stopping points.

To help: Point out various geometric shapes that appear during play with your toddler. Start with circles and ovals, then squares and rectangles, then triangles.

Pictorial drawings. Finally your toddler makes representational drawings of people, animals, houses, and other important things in his life. He now uses art to express himself.

To help: Offer your toddler suggestions. Encourage him to draw a picture of your family, your pet, your house—or a monster!

224. Arts and Crafts Basics

When introducing arts and crafts to toddlers, the process—not the product—is important. Here are some tips to keep in mind.

Supervise. Make sure to supervise your toddler so he doesn't eat anything harmful, hurt himself with any materials, or damage your furniture or floor.

Explore. Offer a variety of arts and crafts materials for him to explore (see Tip 225), so he can investigate their properties, compare and contrast, and experiment with technique.

Don't model. Avoid making models for your toddler to copy, since he won't be able to do it. Let him use his imagination to create whatever he wants.

Simplify. If your toddler seems overwhelmed and is reluctant to explore his arts and crafts materials, simplify things by giving him only one or two materials to try at a time. Show him different ways to use each material, if necessary.

Comment. Avoid evaluative comments. Don't ask your toddler what he's making or tell him it's "the best thing on the planet." Instead, comment on the materials he chooses, the colors he uses, how well he works, and so on.

Display. When your toddler is finished with his artwork, put it on display for all to see. He'll be proud of his work and appreciate your pride in it, too.

225. Make-It-Yourself Craft Kit

Here are some materials and tools to gather and keep in your toddler's craft kit.

- Box to hold the materials
- Colored construction paper
- Colored tissue paper
- Cotton balls
- Craft foam
- Cupcake liners
- Felt
- Glitter glue sticks
- Glue sticks
- Large crayons
- Large washable felt-tip markers
- Magazines
- Old picture books
- Paper bags
- Paper plates
- Pipe cleaners
- Poster board
- Ribbons
- Ruler
- Safety scissors
- Scraps of cloth
- Stickers
- String
- Tape
- Wallpaper samples
- White paper
- Yarn

226. Quick Tip: All-in-One

My son used to have arts and crafts materials all over the house. He never put things away in the same place twice, and he could never find something when he needed it. Finally I put all his supplies in a big plastic bin. He loves his all-in-one craft bin, and cleanup is easy.

—Lin L.

227. Quick Tip: Pocket Fun

I gave my kids aprons with pockets when they were doing arts and crafts. I had them put small art supplies (safety scissors, markers, glue sticks, tape) inside the pockets so the basic tools were always handy. Sometimes I surprised them by adding something new, such as a glitter pen, stickers, or a box of colored pencils, which was always a treat.

—Charles F.

228. Quick Tip: Keeping Control

To help your toddler handle a pencil or marker more easily, buy rubber grips that slide over the ends. The friction of fingers on the rubber helps toddlers hold the pencil or marker so they have more control over it—which really helps develop their fine motor skills.

—Claire J.

229. Arts and Crafts Activities

Arts and crafts activities provide your toddler lots of opportunities to practice finger control, express emotions, and enhance imagination and creativity.

Scribble time. Give your toddler a large sheet of white paper and some large crayons, markers, or chalk. Let him scribble whatever he wants on the paper. Try different types of paper and marking utensils to expand his experiences.

Finger paints. Let your child explore his sense of touch through finger-painting activities. Give him large sheets of slick paper and provide finger paints. Or make vanilla pudding, tint it your toddler's favorite color, and let him finger-paint on wax paper or right on the table.

Poster paints. Set up an easel for your toddler, and let him paint on large sheets of paper using washable poster paints. Cover him with a smock, and cover the floor with newspaper, an old sheet, or a tarp, so you don't have to worry about the mess.

Collages. Cut out magazine pictures and have your toddler glue them on a large sheet of paper in whatever way he wants. Or make a collage out of leaves, scraps of fabric, colored cereals, tinted macaroni, old stamps, postcards, stickers, and other flat objects.

Mosaic. Have your toddler put together a design made from small objects such as bits of colored paper, buttons, tiny candies, seeds, and so on. If he is fairly adept, you might want to outline a simple design first (such as a flower, sun, or sailboat), and encourage him to fill in the sections.

230. Quick Tip:
What Should We Make?

I gave my kids lots of different materials to use, but I never told them what to do. I always left that up to them.

—Melanie E.

231. Quick Tip:
Make It and Stick It

My toddler had a great time making his own stickers. It was great fine motor practice, and we had fun working together on projects. Here's how to do it.

1 packet unflavored gelatin	Small bowl
½ cup boiling water	Sheets of white paper
1 tablespoon sugar	Large crayons
½ teaspoon flavoring, such as vanilla	Scissors
	Small paintbrush

Mix the gelatin with boiling water, sugar, and vanilla in a small bowl, and set it aside to cool. Next, have your toddler draw small colorful pictures on paper using crayons or markers. Cut out the pictures, paint the backs with the gelatin mixture, and set them out to dry. When your toddler is ready to use his stickers, have him lick the backs and apply them to paper.

—Rhys B.

232. Clay and Dough

Working with modeling clay and Play-Doh (or a homemade version) helps all areas of your toddler's development. He increases his fine motor skills by manipulating the material. He uses his cognitive skills by thinking about what he wants to make. And he develops his imagination and emotional skills by sharing his feelings through creative expression.

Snakes and ropes. Show your toddler how to roll out the clay or Play-Doh to make snakes and ropes. Then let him see what he can do with them, such as make a bowl or make a shape.

Pat-a-cakes. Using small chunks of the dough, show your toddler how to pound, pat, and roll the dough into flat circles. Then see what he can do with them, such as stack pancakes, roll up burritos, or cut pizzas.

Cookie cutters. Give your toddler a variety of plastic cookie cutters, and show him how to use them to cut flattened dough. Try other objects, such as plastic cups or glasses, plastic knives, and small box or jar lids. Watch him carefully when he's using potentially dangerous utensils.

Other gadgets. Give your toddler other objects to create things with the dough—such as a colander, garlic press, Popsicle sticks, plastic utensils, measuring spoons, rolling pins, and toy hammers.

233. Quick Tip: Peanut Butter Play Dough

My toddler loved to play with Play-Doh, but he also kept putting it in his mouth. If your toddler likes to eat Play-Doh, here's a recipe for peanut butter play dough that he can play with and munch on, too.

1 cup smooth peanut butter
½ cup honey
1½ cups powdered milk (not instant)

Mix the ingredients in a medium bowl. Place the dough on a table or countertop and knead it well. Add a little powdered milk if it's too sticky, or add a little honey if it's too dry. You want it to have a soft, doughy consistency. Then let the kids play with it. It's no problem if they put a little in their mouths.
—Ann P.

234. Prewriting Practice

Give your toddler prewriting practice by letting him scribble. Scribbling helps him control his hands and fingers, encourages self-expression, and prepares him for writing.

Big size. Offer your toddler large sheets of paper and big washable markers so he's more likely to keep the marks on the paper. As his control increases, give him smaller sheets of paper and smaller markers.

Paper. Give him different types of papers so he can have different scribbling experiences. Give him colored paper, glossy paper, aluminum foil, wax paper, wrinkled paper, textured paper, and so on.

Writing utensils. Let him experiment with different writing and drawing utensils to help him expand his skills. Try fat markers, thin markers, crayons, chalk, black lead and colored pencils, glitter pens, small paintbrushes (with watercolors or poster paints), and finger paints.

Scribble stories. Read a familiar children's story while your toddler scribbles. Change your voice and tempo to match the storyline. Use different voices for the different characters. Sound sad, scared, excited, wishful, and so on. See if your toddler alters how he scribbles during the reading.

Scribble fun. Have your toddler scribble with each hand separately, with both hands at the same time, with his eyes closed, and holding the markers in a variety of creative ways.

235. Hands and Fingers

As your toddler gains control over his arms and legs, he also works on controlling his hands and fingers. Provide him lots of opportunity to practice his fine motor skills through games and activities.

Picking up toys. Help your toddler learn to pick up his toys when he's finished playing. Give him a basket to collect the toys, and large containers to store them in.

Setting and clearing the table. Teach your toddler how to put the silverware on the table and fold and place the napkins. When the meal is over, have him help you remove the dishes carefully and carry them to the kitchen sink.

Cooking. Let your toddler join you while you prepare foods for breakfast, lunch, snacks, and dinner. He can stir, measure, pour, fill, and do all kinds of fine motor tasks under your supervision.

Sorting the laundry. Dump the clean clothes into a big pile and let your toddler sort them according to each family member. Show him how to fold towels, and have him help you put the clothes away.

Button, button. Gather some small items such as buttons, coins, or various pastas, and have your toddler sort them (by color, size, or shape) into an egg carton or small containers. Tell him not to put the objects in his mouth, and keep a close eye on him while he works.

Clothing hunt. In the morning, hide the pieces of your toddler's outfit in plain sight. Have your toddler look for the items and put each one on in order. If he finds his pants before his underpants, he must leave the pants where they are and continue to search for the underpants. Make sure to let him dress himself (or try to) so he gets some fine motor practice. (See Tip 236.)

Puzzle pieces. Buy or make some simple puzzles for your toddler to put together. Make sure the pieces are large, and avoid puzzles over ten pieces. As your toddler's fine motor skills develop, provide puzzles with smaller pieces.

Handy work. Set small toys and plastic bowls on the floor. Have your toddler put the objects in the bowls in the following ways: wearing garden gloves, wearing sock mittens, wearing a puppet, using tongs, scooping with a large ladle, with his eyes closed, with his toes, and so on.

236. Dressing with Success

When your toddler shows signs of wanting to dress himself, it's a step toward independence and a great opportunity for him to hone both his fine and gross motor skills. Here are some tips to help him dress with success.

Self-help skills. Encourage your toddler to do as much as he can. For example, after pulling a T-shirt over his head, coax him to push his arms through the sleeves. See if he can lift each foot so you can put on his socks and shoes. Ask him to hold out his arms as you put on his coat. As he becomes more independent and has more practice, he'll soon be able to manage these skills on his own.

Dress a doll. Give your toddler a large doll and some clothes, and let him practice dressing it.

Start simply. Keep his clothes simple—easy to put on and take off. Avoid complicated zippers, snaps, and fasteners. Stick to elastic and Velcro. Replace snug-fitting clothes with looser ones, and be sure his T-shirts have a large opening for the head. Have him start with simple tasks, such as pulling on pants that have an elastic waistband.

Accept mistakes. If his shirt is inside out or backward, let it go. Praise his success.

237. Quick Tip: Dress the "Hokey Pokey"

My toddler insisted on dressing himself, but he had a lot of trouble getting his legs through the pant legs and his arms through the armholes. Finally I laid the pants on the bed near his feet and showed him how to slip his legs in. Then we made up our own version of the "Hokey Pokey" and sang, "You put your leg in, you put your other leg in, you pull your pants up, and you zip them way up." I did the same thing with his shirt. I laid it facedown on the bed and showed him how to dive into the bottom of the shirt, while singing, "You put your arm in, you put your other arm in." We had a great time together.

—Shi P.

238. Quick Tip: Fashion Plate

We played "fashion designer" with our girls, which gave them plenty of practice dressing themselves. Each night, we selected a few clothing items at random. The next day, they got to put together their outfits with any of those items. Sometimes things matched and sometimes they didn't, but I didn't worry because they loved making their choices and they quickly learned to dress themselves.

—Cindy M.

239. Tying Shoes:
The Bunny Rabbit Method

If your toddler is having trouble learning to tie his shoes, try the bunny rabbit method.

1. Tell your toddler to pretend the laces are bunny ears.
2. Hold the ends of each lace straight up.
3. Cross them over and set them down.
4. Pick up the end of the bottom lace and send it through the "hole" created by the crossed laces.
5. Pick up both laces and pull them tight.
6. Set the laces down again.
7. Make a "bunny ear" by forming a loop with the right lace.
8. Hold on to the "ear" in one hand, and pick up the other lace in the other hand.
9. Cross the other lace over the "ear."
10. Poke the middle of the lace through the "hole."
11. Pull both "ears" to tie the shoe.

240. Quick Tip: Velcro versus Laces

Although my son loved the Velcro fasteners on his shoes because they were fast and easy to use, I wanted to make sure he had the opportunity to learn how to tie shoes. So I bought him both kinds—Velcro and laces—and had him take turns wearing different shoes on different days. I did most of the lacing for him early on, explaining how it was done. Eventually he was ready to try it himself.

—Dana M.

Chapter 12
Cognitive Development

241. Thinking Skills

Toddlers learn cognitive skills through everyday activities such as eating, getting dressed, going to the toilet, brushing teeth, cleaning up toys, and so on. Maria Montessori said children at this age have "absorbent minds," and Jean Piaget called toddlers "little scientists." They're beginning to reason, problem solve, understand cause and effect, and comprehend spatial relationships, math concepts, time, and distance. Through play, your toddler develops skills that lead to higher levels of thinking. Here are some tips for enhancing your toddler's thinking skills throughout the day.

Talk. Chat with your child as much as possible. Engage her in conversations to build her vocabulary, help her use language in creative ways, help her understand concepts, and so on.

Ask questions. Stimulate your toddler's thinking skills by asking her simple questions about what she's doing and the things around her. For example, if she's drinking from a sippy cup, ask her if the color of the lid matches the color of the cup. If they don't, then ask her what colors they are. When she asks you a question, encourage her to think of an answer before you respond.

Give options. Instead of telling your toddler what to do, offer her choices so she can learn to problem solve, understand cause and effect, and increase control over her life. Toddlers have a high need for control—that is, for independence—so giving them options (when possible) helps meet that need.

Try new ways. Encourage your toddler to try new ways of doing things—such as, new ways to comb her hair, get from one place to another, play with a toy, draw a picture, dance and sing, make sound effects, shape Play-Doh—so she can practice thinking creatively.

Teach. Your toddler will frequently want to perform an activity by herself, but sometimes she'll first need you to teach her how to do it. This situation will help her learn to listen and follow directions.

Offer praise and feedback. As your toddler works on a project, reinforce her efforts by saying, "I like how hard you're working," or "You're doing a great job!" so she knows you're watching and that you care.

Work together. Participate in your child's play from time to time. Work together on her projects, activities, and games, so she can learn social skills and new ways to play. Ask her to help you with your projects, too.

Set your toddler up for success. Your toddler needs to succeed often, so make sure her activities aren't beyond her skill level. Succeeding enhances previously learned skills, helps her acquire new skills, and builds her self-confidence. The more your child succeeds, the more she'll try new activities, take risks, and continue to succeed.

242. Quick Tip: Think for Yourself

When my toddler asked a question, I'd say, "What do you think?" I tried to let him figure out the answer first instead of just giving him the quick answer. Sometimes he'd figure it out, and other times he'd make a great creative guess, which always impressed me, too.

—Kelly S.

243. Quick Tip: Enriching Experiences

Read to your toddler at a slightly higher level than you think he's capable of understanding. You'll be surprised at how much he understands. I read my toddler a chapter from an early-reader book each night, then asked him questions about the story to make sure he understood what was happening. He understood most of it, and I explained the parts he didn't get.

—Dana M.

244. Quick Tip: A New Perspective

Stimulate your child's curiosity with a new hands-on experience. For example, when I got my hair cut in a spiky style, I let the kids touch it. They loved the feel of it against their palms. We talked about how it was different from curly hair or flat hair. It was a new experience for them.

—Brian Y.

245. Learning Colors

Learning to recognize and identify colors may seem an easy task since we adults take it for granted. But it's a challenge for a toddler. Here are some ways to help.

Talk about colors. As your child gets dressed or chooses a toy, identify the color as you talk about it. You might say, "You're wearing your green shirt," or "There's your red ball!"

Sort by color. When you're going through a pile of clean laundry, show your child how to sort the clothes by color, beginning with the primary colors (red, yellow, and blue). Then add green, orange, and purple. Sort toys, food, and other objects, too.

Color with crayons. Give your toddler large sheets of paper and a box of eight large crayons or markers (red, yellow, blue, green, orange, purple, white, and black). Talk about the colors as she's drawing.

Read a book. Read books about colors to reinforce what your toddler is learning.

Choose a color day. Let your child choose a favorite color, and designate the day as "Red Day" or "Purple Day." Look for objects with the selected color as you go about your routines and activities.

246. Problem-Solving Skills

One way to help your toddler develop her thinking skills is to offer her problem-solving tasks and activities. Here are some ways to develop your child's problem-solving skills while avoiding frustration.

Set up the problem. Think of simple problems for your toddler to solve, such as putting on her socks, cleaning up toys, brushing her hair, or finding a certain object.

Let your toddler try. You may be tempted to solve your toddler's problem when you're in a hurry or when you think she may become frustrated, but let her try first. You may be surprised at what she can do. Watch her as she works so you can see how she learns (physically, visually, audibly, and so on), then build on her style of learning. Offer her help only if she needs it.

Show her how. If your toddler is struggling with a task, show her how to break it into manageable steps so she can eventually learn to do it herself.

Build on skills. After your toddler solves a problem, offer her a slightly more complicated one that challenges her thinking and builds on her accomplishments. For example, after she can blow bubbles, suggest she catch one on the wand.

Use problem-solving toys. Buy or make toys that involve specific problem-solving activities, such as puzzles, blocks, busy boxes, manipulation boards, sorting games, memory games, and matching games.

Repair something. Ask your toddler to help you repair various objects around the house—for example, a ripped piece of paper, a wet book or magazine, a half-deflated balloon, a stuck jar lid, or a knob that came off a drawer.

247. Quick Tip: Role Model

If your child doesn't seem interested in playing with something such as blocks, sit down and start playing with them yourself. He'll watch you, learn what to do, and will eventually play with them himself. Being a good role model is one of the best ways to develop your child's interest in learning a new skill.

—Isabel L.

248. Memory Games

Your toddler's memory skills are growing rapidly during these early years. She'll need lots of repetition to increase her long-term memory and retrieval skills. Offer her activities and games that will help develop these skills.

What's missing? Set out two toys for your toddler to examine. Tell her to close her eyes, then put one of the toys out of sight. Ask your toddler, "What's missing?" Give her hints if she needs help, such as "It's red" or "It's round." Increase the number of toys as her memory develops.

Follow instructions. Tell your toddler to do two simple tasks, such as "Get the toy and put it in the box." See if she can perform the tasks from memory, then add more tasks as her memory increases.

What happens next? Get out one of your toddler's favorite books that you've read several times. As you read the story, pause before you turn the page. Ask your toddler if she remembers what's going to happen next. Then turn the page to see if she remembered correctly. As her memory increases, try it with a book she's heard less often.

Memory. There are many versions of the children's game Memory, whether you buy or make them. The main idea revolves around a deck of cards made up of different pairs. Place the cards facedown and let your toddler turn up two of them. If they match, she can remove that pair from the group. If they don't match, she turns them facedown and tries to remember their positions Then she turns over two more cards, and so on.

249. Learning Shapes

Although shapes may seem like basic concepts that your toddler will learn naturally, she needs you to name them in order to learn what they are.

Basic shapes. Begin with circles, squares, and triangles, then add rectangles, ovals, stars, crosses, and other common shapes. Cut out the shapes and let your toddler play with them, compare them, match them, and find a specific one.

Round and round. Have your toddler use chalk to draw a large circle on the patio or a cement slab at the park. Or help her make the large circle using masking tape on the carpet. Have her march in a circle by staying on the line. Talk about "round" and "circle." You could also do this with squares, triangles, and other shapes.

Seeing circles. Look around the house and see how many circles you can spot, such as bowls, clocks, lamp shades, balls, and so on. Do the same for squares and other shapes.

Building blocks. Take out your toddler's blocks and have her separate the square ones from the rest of the shapes. Build a square-shaped building using the blocks.

Popsicle stick squares. Have your toddler glue four Popsicle sticks on a piece of paper to make a square, then have her turn the square into a house or building by gluing two more sticks to make a triangular shape for the roof.

250. Counting and Numbers

Toddlers are capable of understanding number concepts, and they're even able to begin counting. Begin by teaching the concept of number one. Once she knows what one means, move to number two and continue on as long as your toddler understands. Here are some tips for teaching number concepts.

Number one fun. As your go about your day, find examples of individual objects and point them out to your toddler. For example, say, "There is one apple," "Here is one cookie," and "Do you want one of these toys?"

One out of many. When you come across a group of objects, say to your toddler, "Here are many, many crayons." Pick one up and say, "And here is one crayon."

Where's the one? Place multiples of several different toys or objects around the room in plain sight. Ask your toddler to find one from each group, using words like, "Can you find one block?" "Can you bring one ball to me?" and so on.

One, two. Introduce the concept of two by giving your child two items, one at a time, and counting them as you do: "One cracker, two crackers" or "One shoe, two shoes." You'll be surprised at how many counting situations you encounter throughout the day.

One or two? Offer your toddler a choice of one or two items. For example, ask her if she wants one or two markers. Then count them out as you give them to her.

How many? Set two toys in front of your toddler, counting them out as you do. Hide one under a towel and ask her how many toys she sees. Reveal the second toy and ask her how many she sees. Count the toys for her, "One, two trucks."

Three's company. After your toddler understands the concepts of one and two, begin to introduce the concept of three and beyond using the techniques above.

251. Math Skills

Although your toddler may not be counting yet, she's beginning to understand math concepts. Here are some games and activities for developing premath skills.

Count one, two, three. Count objects throughout the day with your toddler. For example, "There's one cat" or "One, two, three stickers." Toddlers also love to count stair steps as they climb them.

Size matters. Talk about various sizes with your toddler to make her aware of the concepts. You might say, for example, "Here's my big shoe and your little shoe," "This is a big cookie and that is a little cookie," or "Should we read the little book or the big book?"

Do puzzles. Puzzles help children understand shapes and spatial relationships, which are part of geometry. Begin with simple puzzles that contain only a few pieces. Provide progressively difficult puzzles as your toddler masters the simpler ones.

Work on classification skills. Introduce classification skills by sorting a group of items that have shared characteristics—such as toys, foods, clothing, utensils, and so on. Sort the objects by color, size, shape, and so on. (See Tip 252.)

Play "One Is Missing." Set out three blocks in a row, and count them with your toddler. Remove one block and count the two that are left. Ask her if one is missing. Once she understands the concept, put the missing block back, and together count the three blocks. Then ask her again if one is missing. Repeat, using three different items.

Let's predict. Read a new children's book to your toddler. Pause before turning the page, and ask her, "What do you think will happen next?" Or pause a new children's video, and ask her the same question.

Let's estimate. Once your toddler masters numbers over three, put a few jellybeans or other small items in a clear jar. Ask your toddler to guess how many are in the jar. Mark the height of the jellybeans with a short horizontal line on the jar. Then let your toddler pour them out and count them. Record the total next to the line on the jar. Repeat twice, filling the jar above the first height, and then below it. Then fill the jar to a height between two of the lines. Ask your toddler to estimate the number based on the information she has.

252. Classification Games

Having your toddler group objects into different categories based on their shared traits is one of the most important ways to help her organize and understand her world. Begin sorting according to general traits such as color (see Tip 245) or shape (see Tip 249), then modify the activity using more specific categories. Here are some examples.

Toys. Collect a group of random items, with one-third of them being toys. Have your toddler sort out the toys. When she masters that, move to different types of toys, such as moving toys, hard toys, soft toys, small toys, different-colored toys, and similar-shaped toys.

Animals. Ask your toddler to name as many animals as she can think of. Then have your toddler be more specific by naming animals that are small, large, furry, loud, quiet, and so on. For example, for furry animals she might name squirrels, cats, bears, and rabbits.

Clothing. Begin with general clothing items such as dresses, pants, shirts, and shoes, then move to top clothing and bottom clothing, men's and women's clothing, adults' and children's clothing, each family member's clothing, and so on.

253. Board Games

Older toddlers can be introduced to popular board games appropriate for their age level. Here are some classics.

Chutes and Ladders. This basic game of climbing forward and sliding back is easy to learn and fun for toddlers. They improve their counting skills and fine motor development as they play.

Candy Land. Everyone loves Candy Land because it's such a "sweet" fantasy game! Players match the cards to the spaces on the board.

Hi Ho! Cherry-O. Your toddler will practice her fine motor skills and enjoy the excitement of hanging cherries on the tree.

254. Puzzles and Problems

Play-Doh puzzle. Roll out Play-Doh and cut shapes at least 1 inch apart using cookie cutters. Carefully remove each shape, leaving the rolled-out outline. Have your toddler place the shapes back in the appropriate places, like a puzzle.

Store-bought puzzles. Wooden puzzles come in various themes from animals to food to people. If your toddler has trouble, give her suggestions, but avoid doing the puzzle yourself.

Homemade puzzles. Make your own puzzles using colorful pictures from magazines or picture books. Use spray adhesive to glue the pictures onto heavy poster board or foam board. (Make sure the entire picture sticks to the board.) Then draw large puzzle shapes using a black marker and cut them out. Your toddler can put the shapes back together.

Hands-on problems. Give your toddler a simple problem to solve, such as finding a "missing" toy, putting together a simple build-it-yourself toy, or making a peanut butter sandwich. Give her hints to help her solve the problem herself.

Thought problems. While playing with your toddler, ask her what she would do in certain situations. For example, "What would you do if you got really, really hot?" or "How would you make a peanut butter sandwich if you didn't have any bread?"

255. Quick Tip: Experiments

I wanted my kids to get exposed to thinking scientifically, so I tried to think of a daily experiment for them to do. In one experiment they put drops of food coloring into a platter of milk, then touched the milk with a toothpick coated with a tiny drop of dish soap. In another they put leaves on a piece of dark-colored construction paper, then placed the paper in bright sunlight to see what happened. They loved it.
—Dana M.

256. Same and Different

Play games to get your toddler thinking about classification properties. Here are some to try.

Same-same. Pick out pairs of objects and set one of each around the room. Put the remaining objects in the middle of the room. Show your toddler one object from the middle of the room and have her hunt for the match.

Same-different. Pick out pairs of objects that are similar but not exactly the same. For example, two socks that aren't the same color, two books with different titles, and so on. Have your toddler find the objects that are similar but still different, and talk about their properties.

Different-different. Pick out pairs of objects that are opposites. For example, one white sock and one black sock, a big picture and a small picture, and so on. Have your toddler match the opposites, then talk about how they're different.

257. TV Menu

Television can be a learning tool if used appropriately and in moderation. Here are some tips for selecting programs and setting time limits for your toddler's viewing.

Watch with your child. Watch programs with your child so you can make sure the content is appropriate. You can also answer her questions and comment on things she might not understand.

View from your child's perspective. When you watch a show that your toddler enjoys, try to see it from her perspective. What do you think she likes about the program? What is she learning from it? What might be scaring her? Are there things you can discuss about the show?

Rent educational videos. Instead of watching TV shows, rent videos specifically created for your child's age group. Read the cover notes to determine their educational value.

Spread the word. Once you decide which programs and videos are appropriate for your toddler, prioritize and list them (include the day, time, and channel of the TV shows). Photocopy your list and have it available for babysitters, relatives, and any others who may care for your toddler. You may also want to make a list of shows that are inappropriate for your toddler.

Monitor TV Land. Decide the daily amount of time you'll allow your toddler to watch the approved TV shows. If two hours is the limit, be sure to break it up into at least two segments and schedule other activities between each segment. Watching an hour in the morning and another hour later in the day can be a nice balance with indoor and outdoor play, eating, napping, and so on. Remember, less is more.

258. Quick Tip: Best Videos

My daughter loved to watch videos, and I preferred them to TV shows because their content was usually more educational. She had three favorites that she watched over and over: (1) The Alphabet Zoo *(Mazzarella Bros. Productions). She loved this one because she learned the alphabet by visiting the zoo. (2)* Gullah Gullah Island: Dance Along with Binyah and Friends *(Sony Wonder). This one was great because it featured multicultural kids. (3)* Movin' & Groovin' *(The Learning Station). She loved to sing and dance to this video.*

—Shanice A.

259. Overuse of Video Games, Computers, and TV

Playing video and computer games and watching television can be educational, if done in moderation, but it's easy to overdo it. Doing so leads children to become passive learners rather than active learners. Overusing video games, computers, and TV cuts into your toddler's playtime and may also contribute to oversnacking and lack of exercise. Here are some tips to help break the habit.

How much is too much? If your child engages in the activity for long periods (such as two-to-three hours at a time), that's too much. If she's restless and irritable when she can't continue, that's a sign of a problem. If she always chooses video and computer games or TV over playing with friends, she's going to need some intervention.

Redirection. Distract your toddler from video games or TV by helping her get started on another activity. Suggest an outdoor activity that will increase her gross and fine motor skills—for example, playing ball, running in the sprinkler, marching to music, or staging a mini track meet. Help her rev up her cognitive skills with a favorite puzzle, simple science experiment, or a classification game. Engage her artistic side with finger paints or Play-Doh. Or enhance her social skills by inviting friends over for a cooking experience or game of chase.

Set time limits. If you child loves her video game or TV show, set a firm time limit with an egg timer. When the timer rings, the game or show is over and it's time to do something else.

Avoid adding to the problem. Although it's tempting to use TV or the computer as a babysitter, don't overdo it, especially now. If you need to get something done, synchronize it with an approved electronics period or do it after your toddler is set up in another activity.

Compromise. Tell your toddler that for every half hour of TV she watches or game she plays, she must play outside (or do another activity) for an hour.

Pull the plug. If all else fails, simply turn off the TV, computer, or video game. To be fair, that goes for the whole family, not just your toddler.

260. Quick Tip: Uh-Oh. It's Broken!

My toddler was so addicted to TV, he had a fit every time we turned it off. I think he'd watch it all day if he could. We finally decided we had to do something, even if it meant giving up our own favorite shows. One day the TV just "broke." At first my son was upset, but then he realized there was nothing we could do—it was "broken." He soon found other things to do to keep him engaged, stimulated, and happy. We haven't watched TV in five years and haven't even missed it.

—Ann P.

261. Quick Tip: Computer Fun

As long as they're not overused, computers are great for toddlers. Toddlers easily catch on to using the mouse, and there are lots of on-line activities and games available for them to play, including drawing, painting, and doing puzzles. Try the Sesame Street *site (http://pbskids.org/sesame) for fun activities for your toddler.*

—Susan W.

Chapter 13
Language Development

262. First Words

Around one year of age, your toddler may say his first word. Eventually he'll say several words, and over time he'll begin using two-word phrases and sentences. Children are born with a biological predisposition to acquire language and speech, but they need exposure to language and reinforcement from parents and caregivers to develop their skills. Here are some tips for helping your child increase his language skills.

Talk. Just because your child isn't talking yet doesn't mean he isn't learning language. It's very important to talk (and read and sing) to your child during the preverbal period. Your toddler's ability to understand language far outpaces his ability to speak it. He'll probably understand about fifty words before he says his first word. He needs you to name things he's looking at, to repeat simple sentences often, and to use a high-pitched voice that's more engaging for him to listen to.

Listen. Make sure to give your toddler a chance to talk. Show him how to take turns during "conversations." Listen closely to his vocalizations and reinforce them by nodding your head, smiling, and speaking a few more words. Waiting for his response also tells him that his input matters.

Provide positive reinforcement. Just as it's important to talk to your preverbal toddler, it's equally important to reinforce your child's speech as he begins saying a few words. Responding positively to your toddler each time he speaks will reinforce his desire to speak.

Use body language. Use lots of gestures, body language, and facial expressions while talking to your toddler. Watch his body language, too, when he tries to talk to you. Your toddler will continue to use the gestures (such as pointing) that helped him communicate his needs during the preverbal period.

Watch gender differences. Parents tend to talk to their girls more than their boys, and girls tend to speak earlier than boys. Beware of this so you make sure you're providing sufficient language input to your child.

Promote first words. A toddler's first words typically reflect the things that are most important to him, such as *dada, blankey, juice, doggy, ball,* and so on. You'll know which things are important by observing your child's behavior. If you use the words that name his important things frequently, your toddler may begin using them sooner.

Avoid corrections. Never correct or criticize your toddler's speech, or he may be less inclined to speak. Don't ignore his vocalizations either, or his rate of speech development may be slowed. Simply model the correct pronunciation of words early and often, and he'll acquire speech and language naturally.

263. First Words in Bilingual Families

If your family speaks another language in addition to English, your toddler has a wonderful opportunity to expand his language and cultural horizons. Here are some tips for increasing language development for a bilingual toddler.

Start young. Continue to use both languages from the moment of birth. Even though your toddler isn't speaking much, he absorbs a great deal of language.

Don't laugh. If your toddler attempts to speak either language and makes a mistake, don't laugh or tease him and don't correct him. He may stop talking altogether. Just continue to model the correct pronunciation, and he'll eventually say the words correctly. This way, he'll be less self-conscious and will feel less embarrassed about his mistakes.

Listen up. When your toddler attempts to use either language, listen to him to show him how important his words are. Encourage his use of both languages by praising him, nodding your head, and smiling.

Code-switching. As your toddler experiences another language outside the home, he'll learn to code-switch, meaning, he'll instinctively know when to use his native language (say, at home), and when to use another language (say, at school). Be sure to expose him to many different language situations in and outside of the home.

Be proud. Take pride in speaking your native language (at home and in public) as well as in your ability to use another language. Each language is rich and beautiful and should be a source of pride to you and your toddler.

264. Quick Tip: Bilingual and Bicultural

I wanted my child to learn his native language and English at the same time, so I alternated using Spanish and English when talking to him. I was worried that he might be confused by this, but he picked up both languages quickly and seemed to know that he had to speak Spanish to his grandparents, while his friends only seemed to know English. It amazed me that he knew when to switch languages. I think he was proud to know both languages.

—Gay C.

265. Twin Talk

Twins can be slower to speak than single-born children for a number of reasons. If they have older siblings, the older kids may be more likely to speak for them or finish their sentences. Parents may prolong the use of baby talk, or talk less to their twins individually. If the twins were born premature, their development can be delayed in general. Sometimes the twins reinforce each other's incorrect forms of speech, delaying the need for correct speech. Here are tips to encourage your twins to talk.

One at a time. When you speak to your children, talk to them individually, rather than as a team, so they get direct input from you. Listen to them individually as well, and use each of their names rather than saying "twins."

Speak clearly and slowly. If your twins were born early and have an overall delay in development, speak clearly when you communicate, so they can distinguish the sounds of speech.

Use repetition. All children learn through repetition, so repeat your words and phrases often with your twins. Use gestures or a form of sign language to reinforce the words.

Avoid talking for them. Don't finish their sentences. Be patient and let them get the words out. Otherwise, they may hesitate to speak at all.

Encourage them to talk. Instead of responding to only their gestures, ask, "What do you want?" and encourage them to use words. Reinforce their attempts.

Read to them. Picture books are a great way for all children to learn language, so read to them every night. Ask questions about the story, and encourage them to ask questions, too. Read favorite stories over and over so they hear the rhythm of the language and understand the story through repetition.

Speech delay concerns. If you think your twins have a speech delay beyond the norm (they should be using several words by age two), consult your doctor or a speech therapist to see if there's anything else causing the delay.

266. Quick Tip: Language Crutch

My twin girls were slow to talk other people. Each twin was the other's language "crutch" in social situations. They'd separate themselves from other people and talk only to each other. Before they started preschool, I enrolled the girls in separate art classes so they had a chance to interact with other people. Without her sister there, each twin couldn't rely on her language crutch to avoid talking to others. While the girls were shy and quiet at first, their curiosity about the kids and activities soon got the best of them, and they started talking to people in and out of the classes.
—LaWanda M.

267. Talking to Toddlers

By the end of the first year, your toddler's language skills will increase rapidly. Here are some ways to continue that development.

Chat. Continue having conversations with your toddler about familiar topics throughout the day. Doing so helps him learn new words in context.

Ask questions. Include questions during your chats to elicit your toddler's verbal responses. Occasionally ask open-ended questions that require more than yes-or-no responses. For example, instead of saying, "Do you like red?" say, "What is your favorite color?"

Use creative language. Use interesting and imaginative language with your toddler. Be descriptive, use action verbs, speak in rhymes, and make language fun.

Read. Reading to your toddler is one of the best ways to enhance his language development. Reading often teaches children vocabulary they wouldn't be exposed to otherwise. As you read a story to your toddler, ask him questions about the story line or the illustrations. Repeat a book as many times as your toddler wants—and as you can stand.

Repeat. Toddlers like to hear words and phrases repeated, so say your phrases and short sentences two or three times to help your child learn the words and their meanings. For example, say, "Here's your teddy bear! I found your teddy bear! Your teddy bear was on the floor!"

Expand. When your toddler says a word such as *milk,* repeat the word and expand on it. For example, say, "Would you like some milk?" and "Okay, I'll get you some milk."

Watch baby talk. It's okay if your toddler regresses to baby talk now and then. He may, for example, slur or mispronounce words he knows, use only single words or two-word phrases, or even babble. He's probably just playing with language or pretending to be a baby. However, it's important not to model baby talk for your toddler.

268. Quick Tip: No Baby Talk

A speech therapist once told me that the number one reason why kids are sent to her is because parents use baby talk. She told me a little baby talk is okay when children are just beginning to vocalize in the first year, because imitating their sounds encourages them to vocalize more. However, after a child begins saying his first words, it's important to reinforce the proper forms of language. She told me she often has to "unteach" the baby talk, then teach kids how to speak correctly. She encouraged me to use appropriate words and correct pronunciations when my children were toddlers so there wouldn't be a problem later on.
—Susan W.

269. Quick Tip: Speak Up, Not Down

I think it's important not to talk down to kids. The biggest compliment I got from a child-free friend of mine was that I spoke to my children like they were adults. I explained to her that I saw my kids as people who could understand most of what I said, and that their speech skills would develop as they grew. I also mentioned that I didn't go overboard—that is, use vocabulary and sentence structures clearly too complicated for them. Speaking to children in a mature, respectful manner is good for their self-esteem and their language development.

—Isabel L.

270. Dealing with Swear Words

Even though your toddler doesn't understand what swear words mean, he may notice that people are usually upset or excited when they say them. He may then try out those words as a way to explore his independence. When he says a swear word, he may get an immediate, tense reaction (*"What* did you say?"), which only reinforces the behavior. Here are some tips for dealing with inappropriate language in an appropriate way.

Don't punish. While your instinct may be to lecture or punish your toddler for saying swear words, consider the result. Lectures and punishment probably won't take away the power and mystique of those words. Also, lecturing or punishing your toddler may scare him and break down his trust in you.

Ignore it. Instead of overreacting, ignore the language. It may go away on its own. Your toddler enjoys getting a reaction, even a negative one, so if you ignore the behavior, you don't reinforce it.

Remove the source. Your toddler has heard the word somewhere—perhaps someone in the family, another child, adult, or the television. Try to remove the word at its source so your toddler doesn't hear and use it.

Explain. Tell your toddler the word he used may upset many people, such as grandma or his teacher, and that's why he shouldn't use it.

Confine it to the bathroom. Some parents allow their children to use swear words if they go into the bathroom and close the door. That way they can't upset anyone but can still express themselves.

Be a good role model. Watch your language. Your toddler is listening to you all the time and often copies your language. He's also learning a lot of new words and is prone to picking up these interesting new terms.

271. Word Games and Rhyming

Word games and rhyming are wonderful ways to encourage your toddler's language development.

Body parts. Early on, teach your child the names of his body parts. Then make up a song or chant about each part. Many familiar rhymes and songs teach kids about body parts, including "Head, Shoulders, Knees, and Toes." Toddlers are delighted when you touch each body part as you chant.

Telephone! Get some toy phones and have an imaginary conversation with your toddler.

Rhyme time. Toddlers love the sounds of language, and rhymes call attention to those wonderful sounds. Read nursery rhymes and poetry. Make up your own rhymes throughout the day by saying things like, "Zoom! Zoom! Here comes the broom!" or "Is a yummy in your tummy?" Or play I Say, You Say. Your toddler could say, "I say run, you say–" and you could provide the rhyming word (*bun, sun, fun* and so on).

272. Hearing Concerns

A newborn's hearing is normally screened shortly after birth. However, if your toddler experiences repeated ear infections or fluid buildup in his ears, his hearing may be temporarily impaired. This could affect his language development. Here are some things to watch for.

Hearing difficulties. Does your toddler turn toward unexpected sounds? Does he startle at loud sounds? Does he seem to understand and respond to your speech? If not, talk to your doctor.

Ear infections. Check with your doctor if your toddler has had several ear infections, allergies, or respiratory infections. If there's persistent fluid in your child's ears, your doctor may recommend a hearing test and/or that you see a specialist to check the ears' passageways. Under certain circumstances, your doctor may recommend that ventilation tubes be placed temporarily in your toddler's ears. Early intervention is key to resolving hearing problems and to preventing avoidable language delays.

273. Easing Language Difficulties

Acquiring language is a monumental task that takes several years. You should expect a few difficulties along the way as your toddler builds his vocabulary and learns appropriate pronunciations, meanings, and grammar. You may even see difficulties such as occasional stammering and stuttering. Most of these are normal. Here are some guidelines to help ease his difficulties.

Model correct language. Using the correct forms over and over is the best way to help your child acquire language. Talk to him about what he's doing, what you're doing, where you're going, and so on. When he tries to say something, react enthusiastically and model the correct form. For example, if your child says, "Wan ju-ju," say, "You want some juice?"

Name it. Give him the words he needs to express his thoughts and feelings. Name the toys he plays with, the food he eats, colors, animals, and so on.

Don't interrupt. Don't interrupt your toddler while he's trying to talk. Listen attentively and encourage him with nods and expectant facial expressions. Interrupting just causes him to lose ground (and sometimes confidence) with whatever he's struggling to say.

Don't pressure. Listen patiently and give your toddler time to get the words out. If you look impatient, tell him to hurry up, or complete his sentences for him, he may become self-conscious and be less inclined to speak.

Don't criticize and correct. Avoid saying "No, no! You say it like this..." when your toddler says something incorrectly. Also, don't allow older siblings and others to tease him about his speech. Just let him get the words out in whatever fashion, nod your approval, and say, "Yes." Then model the appropriate speech in a casual, matter-of-fact way. Doing this doesn't mean you approve his mistakes; it means you approve his desire and attempt to communicate.

Try to avoid saying "What?" If you don't understand your toddler, say "Pardon me?" or ask him to expand his words by saying "Tell me more."

Relax. Most language and speech problems are minor and will correct themselves over time.

Check with your doctor. Don't hesitate to talk to your doctor if you suspect your child has a language problem that requires professional attention. Call if your toddler isn't putting a few words together by age two, if his stammering or stuttering worsens, or if anything else about his speech concerns you. Your doctor may check your child's hearing and may refer him to a speech-language pathologist for further evaluation. If your child seems frustrated at his inability to communicate, discuss this with your doctor as well. Early diagnosis and treatment of language delays and other speech problems is important.

274. Finger Play for Young Toddlers

Want to charm your little one? Add "finger play" (movements of the fingers, hands, and arms that highlight spoken words) to your rhymes. Here are some of the classic finger plays for a young toddler.

This Little Piggy

This little piggy went to market. [wiggle big toe]
This little piggy stayed home. [wiggle next toe]
This little piggy had roast beef. [wiggle next toe]
This little piggy had none. [wiggle next toe]
And this little piggy cried, "Wee, wee, wee,
*   all the way home!"* [wiggle baby toe]

Eensy Weensy Spider

The eensy weensy spider went up the water spout
    [turn thumb of one hand toward index finger
    of the other and twist them upward]
Down came the rain [wiggle fingers downward]
And washed the spider out [wave hands outward]
Out came the sun [use arms to form a circle]
And dried up all the rain [pat the air]
And the eensy weensy spider went up the spout again
    [twist thumb and index finger upward again]

Where Is Thumbkin?

Where is thumbkin? Where is thumbkin?
   [hide thumbs inside fingers]
Here I am! Here I am! [hold up thumbs]
How are you today, sir? [bend thumb toward other hand]
Very well, I thank you. [bend other thumb toward first thumb]
Run away! Run away! [hide both hands behind back]

Repeat with the following:
- *Where is pointer?* [use index finger]
- *Where is tall man?* [use middle finger]
- *Where is ring man?* [use ring finger]
- *Where is pinkie?* [use baby finger]

275. Finger Play for Older Toddlers

Older toddlers love finger play, too. Adding movements helps them learn the words of songs and rhymes and increase their language skills. Plus, they are lots of fun!

Wheels on the Bus

The wheels on the bus go round and round
Round and round, round and round
The wheels on the bus go round and round
All through the town [turn hands in a circle]

Repeat with the following:

- *The people on the bus go up and down*
  [stand up and sit down]
- *The doors on the bus go open and shut*
  [open and close hands]
- *The driver on the bus says "Move on back"*
  [wave arm over shoulder]
- *The wipers on the bus go* swish, swish, swish
  [bend elbows and wave upper arms back and forth]
- *The horn on the bus goes* beep, beep, beep
  [make beeping sound]
- *The babies on the bus go "Wha-wha-wha"*
  [use a nasal tone]
- *The kids on the bus say, "This is fun!"*
  [clap and smile broadly]

I'm a Little Teapot

I'm a little teapot short and stout [stand up tall]
Here is my handle [put hand on waist]
Here is my spout [stick other arm out straight to the side]
When I get all steamed up I just shout [shape hand at mouth]
Tip me over and pour me out! [bend to the spout side, pretending to pour]

Five Little Monkeys

Five little monkeys [hold up five fingers]
Swinging in a tree [swing hand back and forth]
Teasing Mr. Alligator [open and close hands like an alligator mouth]
"You can't catch me!" [point to yourself]
Along comes Mr. Alligator [open and close hands slowly]
Quiet as can be [open and close hands more rapidly]
Snap! [clap hands once, loudly]

Repeat with the following:
- *Four little monkeys* [hold up four fingers]
- *Three little monkeys* [hold up three fingers]
- *Two little monkeys* [hold up two fingers]
- *One little monkey* [hold up one finger]

276. Prereading Skills

Your toddler needs to develop skills that prepare him to learn how to read. Prereading skills include listening attentively to the story line of a children's book, having an interest in learning the names of letters, and increased visual perception and memory. Here are some tips to help your toddler prepare for reading.

Read to your toddler. Read a children's book (or preferably several books) to your child each day. Picture books are especially good because they give your toddler a visual image of the words he's hearing. Make reading time fun by using different voices as you read and by asking your child questions about what's going to happen next. By reading good stories to your toddler, he'll add to his language and be more motivated to learn to read.

Keep books handy. Provide your toddler with lots of books to look at and enjoy on his own. Board books and hardcover picture books are best. You can buy your own collection or check them out from your local library. As your toddler handles and explores the books, he will notice that books are fun and interesting.

Act it out. After you read a story with your toddler, have him think about what might happen after the story ends. What might the characters do next? Help your toddler act out parts of the story to make it come even more alive for him. Using props, costumes, and puppets can add more fun to the mini-play.

Make up stories. You don't need a book to enjoy storytelling and build vocabulary. Just make up stories together, and see where they lead.

Stretch his memory. Help your toddler extend his memory by asking questions about his recent experiences, rereading his favorite books, and playing memory games. (See Tip 248.)

Take field trips. Take your toddler around the neighborhood and beyond for some new experiences. Go to the zoo, aquarium, park, animal farm, art gallery, and so on. Talk to him about what you see, so he adds new words to his vocabulary and enriches his awareness.

Continue to chat. Just talking with your toddler throughout the day will help develop his prereading skills. Talk about topics that interest him, ask him about his day, tell him about your day, explain something new, and encourage him to think about new ideas.

Sing songs. Have fun with language by singing songs, reciting poems, chanting, and playing word games. (See Tip 271.)

Offer stories on tape. Let your toddler listen to stories on tape, and tape yourself while reading, too.

277. Quick Tip: Play It Again

Every time I read a new story to my son, I record it on a cassette player so he can listen to it again and again. He has several tapes of his favorite fairy tales and stories, and he loves to hold the book while listening to the story. It makes him feel as if he's actually reading.

—Dana M.

278. Quick Tip: Bedtime Stories

All I can say is read, read, and read some more to your child. Let him pick out his favorite books, and read them over and over. Kids love repetition. It's how they learn vocabulary, grammar, and prereading skills. Eventually he'll have his favorite books memorized and be able to recite them by heart!

—Isabel L.

279. Quick Tip: Spelling Fun

Those magnetized letters people put on their refrigerators are great for teaching simple words to your kids. During meal prep time, I would teach my kids to spell their names or their favorite word of the day. Then we would spell the name of the toddler who was to help set the table and the one who was supposed to help clear. They loved this, and soon they were learning their letters and putting words on the fridge themselves.

—Cindy M.

Chapter 14
Psychological Development

280. Building Self-Identity and Self-Esteem

Your toddler gains a sense of her own identity as she plays alone, learns personal details about herself, interacts with other people, and takes steps toward independence. Her sense of self-worth and self-esteem come gradually from within herself. You cannot build her self-esteem for her, but you can encourage and facilitate by helping her succeed and by showing your love, support, and respect. Here are some tips for nurturing your child's self-identity and self-esteem.

Get personal. As you chat with your toddler, tell her how old she is, where she lives, and so on. Teach her about the valued role she plays in the family and other important details of her life.

Allow ownership. Let your child know that some things are hers—her toys, her clothes, her bed, her stuffed animals, her tricycle, and so on. This knowledge gives her a sense of ownership and power, which contributes to her sense of self. Once she understands ownership, she'll be more apt to share her things with others.

Watch her. Your toddler loves it when you watch her perform, so give her your full attention when she's practicing a skill, performing a task, trying something new, or simply hamming it up. You are her favorite audience.

Praise her actions. Throughout the day, look for the positives in your toddler's behavior. Let her know when she's making progress and that you're proud of her. Whenever possible, avoid vague, general praise and praise directed to her as a person; instead, make your praise specific and relevant to her actions. For example, instead of saying, "That's great!" or "What a good girl!" when she puts on her shoes, say, "Wow! You put on your shoes all by yourself! That's wonderful!"

Avoid overpraising. Guard against going overboard with praise. Toddlers can sense when praise is insincere or inappropriately placed. She may then be confused, and her trust in you may weaken. Overpraising can also lead a child to become a perfectionist and to think she's a failure when she does not hear praise.

Set up successes. The more opportunities your toddler has to succeed at tasks, the more confidence she'll have in her abilities and the more her self-esteem will grow. Set up challenges that encourage her to push her skills to the next level, but make sure she has a good chance of succeeding. Do this by knowing what your toddler can and cannot do and by not setting the bar too high.

281. Self-Esteem Builders

You can nurture your toddler's self-esteem while you go about your everyday activities. Here are a few examples to keep in mind.

Use your child's name. Name recognition is one of the first ways your toddler forms a sense of who she is. Use her name frequently and talk about her in a positive way. Make up games featuring her name, add her name to songs, write her name on the front pages of her books, put her name on her door, and be sure to add her name to her artwork.

Display her projects. Hang up your toddler's artwork and other accomplishments, and display photos of your toddler engaged in various activities. Talk about them with others so your toddler knows you're proud of her.

Give her chores. Your toddler will feel a sense of belonging and competence if you let her contribute to the household by doing simple chores. For example, she can put napkins on the table, fill the dog's bowl, or put away her toys. Find a few chores she can do daily or weekly, and soon she'll know you count on her. Knowing that she's accomplished something useful will promote her self-esteem.

282. Quick Tip: Building Self-Esteem

I don't think we can give our kids self-esteem. But we can give them opportunities to build self-esteem by overcoming obstacles. Self-esteem has to be earned.

—Tracy A.

283. Quick Tip: King for an Hour

About once a month my son and I sit down at the table and make a crown out of construction paper. I cut it out and he decorates it with stickers, felt pens, glitter, fake jewels, whatever we happen to have in the craft kit. Then we crown him "King for an Hour," and I let him take charge (within reason, of course). He has a ball with this make-believe fantasy—who wouldn't? I think it's great for his self-esteem.

—Susan W.

284. Building Trust

According to Erik Erikson, if a child's need for food, safety, warmth, and affection are met in the first few years of life, she'll develop trust with her parents, caregivers, and others, which will continue with future relationships. Here are some tips for helping your toddler build trust.

Be there for your child. Respond to her needs quickly, especially when she's upset, and she'll learn that you're there for her and that she can rely on you.

Be honest with your child. Tell her the truth and explain situations in a simple manner so she understands and believes what you say. Don't tell a falsehood, thinking it will be easier on your toddler. When she finds out you lied, her trust in you will be shaken.

Prepare your child. Anticipate change and think about it from her point of view. If you have to leave her with a babysitter, tell her ahead of time so she's prepared. Tell her where you're going, when you'll be back, and what she'll be doing with the sitter while you're gone. Then return when you say you will.

Protect your child from failure. Don't put more responsibility on your toddler than she can handle, and don't ask her to do things unless you are fairly sure she can do them. If she falls short, she may wonder why you urged her on in the first place, and her trust in you will suffer.

Keep your promises. If you tell your child you'll do something, live up to that promise. She'll lose trust in you if you continually disappoint her. If you can't promise something, tell her the truth—that you'll do the best you can.

Trust your child. Helping your toddler learn a new skill—and then letting her do it by herself—lets her know that you trust her. If your toddler tells you something, trust her. In these and similar ways, your child will learn about trust from her own point of view.

285. Quick Tip: A Promise Is a Promise

It's important that you stick with the promises–good or bad–you make to your children. If I promise my son ice cream after school, I always follow through. If I say he'll go to his room if he doesn't stop throwing toys, I follow through. I think doing this really helps develops a strong sense of trust.
—Susan W.

286. Quick Tip: Broken Promise

I never make a promise I can't keep. My parents promised me a trip to Disneyland for my fourth birthday and then changed their minds. They never told me why. I was devastated. I'd told all my friends and was so excited. I'll never do that to my kids.

—Mary W.

287. Gender Differences

Even as toddlers, boys and girls have different behavioral tendencies and interests. These tendencies are partly innate, but they can also be influenced by the children's environment and by the kind of parenting they receive. Here are some tips for recognizing gender differences and for helping your toddler experience a wide range of opportunities.

Motor skills. Boys tend to prefer vigorous outdoor play and usually have better gross motor skills, while girls tend to like quiet indoor play and usually have better fine motor skills. Encourage your daughter to explore the outdoors by playing ball or climbing at a park, and encourage your son to try some quiet activities such as puzzles and arts and crafts. This way, boys and girls will both increase their gross motor and fine motor skills.

Emotions and nurturing. Girls tend to cry more, show their emotions more, and be more nurturing. But with more dads taking care of babies and toddlers today, your son will see positive modeling of males giving affectionate care and attention. Avoid giving your son the impression that he shouldn't cry just because he's a boy. Encourage him to express his emotions (see Chapter 15) and to nurture younger toddlers, babies, pets, and so on.

Competitive play. Boys tend to prefer competitive, action-oriented play, while girls tend to prefer noncompetitive, language-oriented play. Encourage your son to play house, school, or office, which are noncompetitive and require more language use; encourage your daughter to run races, play chase, or battle monsters, which draw out her competitive, action-oriented skills.

Toys and activities. Most boys prefer "boy toys" such as balls, trucks, and action figures, and "boy activities" such as playing monster games and sports. Most girls prefer "girl toys" such as dolls and dollhouses, and "girl activities" such as playing house and dress-up. Encourage your sons and daughters to enjoy both types of toys and activities so they are presented with a wide range of opportunities to learn new skills.

288. Birth Order

The importance of birth order has been debated for years. Is there really such a thing as "middle-child syndrome" or "baby of the family"? Here's the latest info on birth order and how it may affect your child.

Individuals. First and foremost, your child is an individual. Although she may have some of the characteristics defined by birth order, she is also her own person affected by her inborn nature and her external environment. Birth order simply gives us insight into possible behavior tendencies. If your child tends to be shy or aggressive, you may want to deal with the behavior, no matter what her birth order is.

Variables. Don't just blame a behavior on birth order. Behavior characteristics can also be affected by the number of children in a family, how far apart in age they are, gender, physical differences, disabilities, divorce, unusual circumstances like a death in the family, and so on.

Firstborn Characteristics. The "leader" of the family tends to be responsible, organized, determined, a goal setter, a high achiever, a perfectionist, and detail oriented. These tendencies apply to an only child as well as a firstborn.

Middle-Born Characteristics. The "middle kid" tends to be flexible, generous, social, diplomatic, peacemaking, and competitive. She tends to cooperate, negotiate, and compromise well, and she tends to be less demanding.

Last-Born Characteristics. The "baby" of the family tends to be outgoing, creative, humorous, a risk taker, and an idea person. She also tends to be very affectionate, uncomplicated, and motivating.

289. Quick Tip: Middle Kid

I was a middle-born kid, which I didn't like growing up. I felt lost in the shuffle between my older sister, who got everything first, and my baby brother, who was treated like a little prince. I seemed to be the one who was ignored, maybe because I was so easygoing. Now that I have my own middle-born child, I try to give her special attention to make up for the differences in birth order. Sometimes she gets to go first. Sometimes she gets the special treatment. And sometimes I realize being a middle kid made me what I am today—easy to get along with and sensitive to others.
—Stefan C.

290. The Only Child

If you've decided your toddler is going to be an only child, don't worry about the stereotypes of the "lonely, spoiled brat." Research shows that an only child tends to have lots of advantages over a child who has siblings. Here are some tips for enhancing those advantages.

The only child tends to be more creative. Give your only child many opportunities to express her imagination and creativity through art, music and dance, and dramatic play.

The only child tends to be more verbal. With no siblings, the only child hears mostly adults speaking, so her vocabulary and language skills tend to flourish. Help her expand her sentences and challenge her with new words.

The only child tends to be more social with adults. Your only child interacts mostly with the adults in her home, so she may be quite comfortable around other adults. But since she doesn't have siblings, give her time with other kids so she can continue to develop her social skills.

The only child tends to be more independent. To encourage her independence, let your only child do as much as she can on her own. For example, let her feed herself, dress herself, brush her teeth, and clean up her toys herself.

The only child tends to have higher cognitive skills. Being mostly with adults gives your child a rich input of ideas, and your only child's thinking skills will naturally increase. Give her simple problems to solve early on and ask her opinion about things.

291. Me Do it!

Toddlers want desperately to do things for themselves—and it's perfectly normal. Although your toddler's budding independence will sometimes strain your patience, allow her to do things for herself as much as possible. Here are some tips to keep in mind.

Try simple steps. Break tasks into simple steps so your toddler has a greater chance of achieving her goal. If the task is too complicated, she may get frustrated and quickly give up. Remember, you want her to succeed, so wait until she masters a step before adding another.

Work together. When your toddler is trying something new and challenging, offer to work with her, but make sure you don't take over. Let her do most of the work and only intervene when she needs you.

Allow time. Your toddler moves slowly when figuring out a task, and she needs to repeat it in order to learn it. Allow extra time so she can enjoy the process and not become frustrated.

Emphasize process, not product. As your toddler works on a task, don't worry about the outcome. Let her focus on developing the skills needed to complete the task. If she doesn't achieve her goal right away, you'll be able to discuss ways to enhance the needed skills.

292. Quick Tip: I Think I Can

*My two-year-old always insisted on doing things himself,
even when he needed help. He should have worn a T-shirt
that said "I Can Do It!" on the front and "Mommy Help Me!"
on the back. I tried not to intervene until he showed signs
of becoming frustrated, but those weren't always apparent.*

—Dana M.

293. Quick Tip: Let Your Toddler Try

*Many parents don't realize that their toddlers can do a lot
more than they give them credit for. I say if your toddler
wants to do something, why not let him? Just offer a little
guidance when it's needed. I let my son get in and out of
the car by himself (while I
was standing near him), and
he was proud of that. Most
kids can do many things by
themselves, but their parents
insist on helping them.*

—Susan W.

294. Fostering Independence

As your toddler becomes more skilled at performing her own tasks, offer her specific self-help skills to practice.

Clothing. Lay out your toddler's clothes so she knows what goes on first. For example, lay her underpants facedown on the bed so they're ready to put on. Teach her that the tag goes in back. Make sure to give her articles of clothing that are easy to put on and take off. (See Tip 236.)

Food. Cut your toddler's food into bite-size pieces so it's ready to eat. Give her easy-to-grasp silverware created especially for toddlers, so she can manage the utensils herself. Fill her cup less than half full so she's less apt to spill. Give her a napkin to wipe her face, and occasionally remind her to use it.

Personal hygiene. Help your toddler learn to brush her teeth, wash her face, clean her body in the tub, and comb her hair. She'll feel more grown-up and in control of her life, which will enhance her self-esteem.

Cleanup. Have your toddler clean up after herself by bringing her empty plate to the sink, throwing her dirty clothes into the hamper, and putting her toys away when she's finished playing. If she doesn't want to clean up or if the task seems overwhelming, work together to make the task easier and more fun.

295. Quick Tip: Toddler's Choice

Every once in a while, I let my toddler make an important choice, so he knows his opinion matters. For example, sometimes I let him choose what we'll have for dinner. Or I'll let him choose where we go for our special time that day. He just beams when he makes decisions and we carry them out.

—Jake B.

296. Quick Tip: Let Your Toddler Choose

On days when my daughter didn't have to go to preschool or church, I let her pick out her clothes. She could choose anything she wanted. On preschool days, I selected two outfits and let her choose which one she wanted to wear. That way she still got to choose, but I got to make sure she wore something appropriate for the weather. Once she made her choice, she was eager to put it on herself.

—Dana M.

297. Slow to Warm Up

Some toddlers dive into new things readily. Caregivers may even have to slow them down to keep them out of danger or trouble. But if your toddler is slow to warm up to new activities, new people, or new experiences, allow her to take her time. There's no need to rush her into something she's not sure about. Instead, give her the opportunity to explore things at her own pace, encourage her gently, and praise her as she takes each new step.

Talk about it first. If you want your toddler to try a new experience or activity, talk about it first so she has a clear idea of what's ahead. Ask her questions to make sure she understands or see if she has questions of her own.

Approach slowly. Introduce the situation or activity slowly so she can study it at a safe distance. Then let her explore it on her own terms so she can become familiar with it in a comfortable manner.

Demonstrate. Show her how the situation or activity works. This way she'll see that it's safe and that you enjoy it, too. She may want to enjoy it vicariously before she gets involved.

Invite and encourage. Ask your toddler if she'd like to try the activity, meet the person, or go into the situation. Encourage her to explore it, and stay by her side, if necessary, so she feels safe and secure.

Step by step. Show your toddler how to get involved by taking things one step at a time. If it's a new toy, show her one simple way to play with it. If it's an activity, show her the first step. Let her get comfortable before taking the next step.

Step back. When your toddler becomes involved with an experience or activity, praise what she's doing, and then step back and let her enjoy it on her own. Stay nearby in case she has questions or concerns, and return often to check on her progress and give her further praise.

298. Happy Birthday!

An important part of your toddler's self-esteem and self-awareness is the celebration of her birthday. By two years of age, she's old enough to enjoy a birthday party with a few friends and family, and she'll enjoy it almost as much as you will.

Plan. Plan the birthday celebration step by step. Jot down the guest list, pick out invitations, think about decorations, plan the food, and prepare age-appropriate activities. Let your toddler help whenever possible.

Theme. Let your toddler pick a theme, or choose one that you know she'll like, such as dinosaurs.

Guest list. It's a good idea to keep the guest list fairly small. You might invite only one or two of your toddler's friends, their parents, and a few relatives. Too many guests may overwhelm your toddler.

Timing. Keep the party short—about an hour or an hour and a half—so the length and excitement of the celebration don't wear out your toddler. Plan the party well before or soon after naptime so your toddler is more alert.

Activities. Plan a couple of fun activities for the kids, such as playing with Play-Doh, building castles in the sandbox, running through the sprinkler, making toy houses with blocks, or doing a simple arts and crafts project. Most toddlers are still too young for organized games, but they'll enjoy playing together.

Refreshments. No party is complete without birthday cake and ice cream, but don't expect the young guests to eat much. Include some healthy snacks to keep them energized and to reduce the effect of the sugar. Make the snacks bite-size, and have the kids eat at the table. Be sure to find out ahead of time if any of the guests have food allergies.

Presents. Most guests will want to bring your child a present. To balance that and make it fun for everyone, give the guests favors (stickers, mini boxes of raisins, small packs of crayons, and so on) at various points in the party—for example, when they first arrive, after each activity, after refreshments, and when it's time to go home. Give the guests small paper bags to stow their favors in during the party.

299. Quick Tip: Party Plans

My daughter was so excited about her birthday party. I thought it would be the best day of her life. We invited all her cousins and all her friends from play group. We even hired a clown. But when the party began, she started crying and didn't want to share her toys or do any of the activities. I realized the whole thing was too much for her. I felt so bad. From that day on we kept her parties small, short, and sweet, which worked better for everyone.

—Susan A.

300. Quick Tip: The Birthday Ps

We kept our kids' birthday parties simple. Basically, my girls believed the key to any successful party was the three Ps—popcorn, piñata, and presents. That made it easier for everyone, especially me, and the kids were happy as can be.
—Dana M.

301. Quick Tip: Best Birthday Party

The best birthday party I ever had for my three-year-old was an arts and crafts birthday with three of his best friends. It kept the kids busy, they had fun, and they took home their crafts when they were finished. I even let them decorate their own cupcakes as an activity.

—Kris N.

302. Make a "Me Book"

Your toddler continues to develop her identity through play, interaction with others, body awareness, and independence. Enhance her self-awareness by making a Me Book that features her favorites. Here are some tips to get started.

Cover. Make a cover out of poster board to protect the Me Book. Use two 8½-by-11-inch sheets, and punch three holes along the left side. Glue a close-up picture of your toddler on the front.

Paper. Buy a package of 8½-by-11-inch colored construction or scrapbook paper. Punch holes to match the holes in the cover sheets. Place paper between the cover sheets and tie them together with yarn or twine.

Photos. Select pictures of your toddler from birth to the present and include them in order in the Me Book. Ask your toddler to make a comment about each photo, then record it next to the photo.

Drawings. Collect your toddler's drawings and include them in the Me Book. Write a caption for each picture. Have your toddler draw some pictures specifically for the book.

Mementos. Add small mementos from special occasions, such as birthday cards, toy wrappers, favorite cereal labels, bookmarks, artwork, and so on.

Stickers. Let your toddler put her favorite stickers throughout the book.

Magazine pictures. Let your toddler choose pictures she likes from magazines, and glue them in the Me Book. Ask your toddler to tell you why she likes the pictures, and write down her comments.

Chapter 15
Emotional and Social Development

303. Emotions: From Delight to Frustration to Pride

Your toddler's emotions—which can shift radically even from minute to minute—show how he reacts to his physical condition, his environment, and the people in it. You'll need to recognize your toddler's emerging feelings in order to be sensitive and responsive to them. Here are some of the emotions your toddler will experience.

By age one. Your baby's emotions are recognizable within a few weeks after birth. At first your baby cries to show distress or fear. He may also relax his face to show contentment. By 6 weeks your baby shares a social smile with you. At 3 months he's apt to laugh out loud, frown to show interest, or looked wide-eyed when he's curious. At 4 months your baby can get angry, an emotion that is often triggered by frustration. Between 9 and 14 months your baby may show signs of fear—fear of strangers or fear of separation from you. By 18 months, he's capable of expressing pride, shame, embarrassment, even guilt.

By age two. Your toddler feels insecure at times and in need of your reassurance. As he feels more and more attached to you, he'll express his affection with lots of hugs and kisses. Intense feelings of frustration appear when he fails at a task or doesn't get his way. His emotional willfulness and stubborn negativity may concern you, but his feelings of surprise, excitement, happiness, and sheer delight in everyday things will make you smile.

By age three. Your toddler's emotions increase in number and become deeper and more sophisticated. He feels love and joy, fear and anger. He feels sad, hurt, and lonely at times and may soon begin to feel empathy toward others. He also shows feelings of contentment, disappointment, pleasure, worry, annoyance, jealously, and pride.

304. Quick Tip: Giggle Time

When my son was feeling kind of low, we'd talk about his sadness for a little while, and then we'd have "Giggle Time." I'd get a special scarf, throw it up in the air, and tell him to laugh and giggle until the scarf hit the ground. Then he'd have to stop laughing and try to keep a straight face. It always worked. After a few rounds, he'd be in a much better mood.

—Kristin L.

305. Emotions: How to Respond

Each toddler's emotional development is unique. In many ways, his emotional development intertwines with his language and social development. How can you best support your toddler's evolving emotions? How can you help him express and cope with his emotions? Here are some tips for responding positively to your toddler's feelings.

Name the emotions. Before your toddler can recognize or talk about his emotions, he needs to know what they are called. Be sure to name your toddler's feelings as they come up. You might say, "My, what a big smile! You must feel happy right now" or "Your body is so stiff. Are you feeling scared of that big dog over there?" Name your own emotions for him as well.

Play "I'm a happy face." Call out the game title and then make a happy face. Have your toddler copy you. Do the same for other emotions like sad, mad, surprised, and so on. Later, have him go first and then copy him.

Read stories about feelings. Read to your toddler some of the many children's stories that focus on feelings. Stop reading at various points and ask, "How do you think this person is feeling?" or "How would you feel if something like that happened to you?"

Provide comfort and reassurance. When your toddler is very disturbed and crying, hold and cuddle him as you talk about his feelings. If handy, wrap him in a blanket for extra security. Let him know you empathize with his problem. Reassure him by saying everything will be okay, that you'll take care of him, and that you love him.

Let him cry it out. Crying often helps relieve pent-up tension, and crying may be the only way your toddler can release his frustration. Allow your toddler to cry as you comfort him and talk to him.

Validate. Never negate your toddler's feelings or tease him out of them. His feelings are real, so let him express them and not feel bad about having them. Avoid saying things like "Don't feel sad" or "Big kids don't cry." Suppressing feelings is unhealthy and may lead to psychological problems or the inappropriate expression of feelings later on.

306. Quick Tip: Crying Bear

Whenever my son was upset and crying, he'd get his teddy bear and cuddle it. We started calling it the "crying bear." I would get it for him when he was tired or sad or upset, and he would cry into it. I told him his crying bear was taking in all his tears so he would feel better. That seemed to soothe him for a long time. After he started talking, he began sharing his feelings with his bear. I thought this was a great way for him to learn to express his emotions.

—Rochelle K.

307. Why Toddlers Get Upset

Many times your toddler will seem to get cranky out of the blue. What happened? Here are some common reasons why toddlers get irritable and how you can help.

Changes. Toddlers often break down when their routines are disrupted. Try to keep a regular schedule as much as possible. If change is unavoidable, try to prepare your toddler for what's going to happen each step of the way.

Fatigue. Toddlers get irritable when they're tired. Make sure your child gets a nap, some rest, or quiet time during the day, and maintain a regular bedtime.

Hunger. Toddlers get cranky when they're hungry. This situation is easy to overlook because (1) you're probably not hungry, and (2) toddlers never look hungry. Make sure your child gets frequent snacks and regular meals.

Disappointment. Toddlers get upset when they experience a disappointment, such as not getting a toy, not seeing a friend, or not being able to stay up late. If a disappointment is unavoidable, try to prepare him by talking about it. If he's already disappointed, empathize with him as you as you talk about it.

Lack of verbal skills. Some children are frustrated at their inability to use words to say how they're feeling. Continue to name emotions for your toddler and continue to help him develop his language skills (see Chapter 13). Be patient and encouraging when he tries to describe how he's feeling.

Failure. Toddlers get frustrated and mad when they try to do something and struggle or fail. Help your toddler succeed by giving him manageable tasks, and encourage him to try again.

308. Quick Tip: Why the Crabby Mood?

I've found that crabby moods, negativity, and temper tantrums are often simply a result of kids being hungry. They don't realize when they're hungry, and it manifests in disruptive behavior. If you want to prevent a lot of unnecessary problems, don't forget snack time at home and don't leave the house without snacks and drinks.

—Claire J.

309. Expressing Anger

Everyone feels anger, and toddlers are no exceptions. Like other emotions, anger is not good or bad; it is simply a feeling. Feelings, however, can be expressed in both constructive and destructive ways. Toddlers get angry quickly and act it out impulsively because they haven't learned to monitor their feelings or think about the consequences of their actions. Here are some tips to help your toddler express his anger in safe and appropriate ways.

Use words. Your toddler has (or will soon have) enough language skills to express his anger in words instead of actions. Give him simple phrases such as "I'm mad!" or "I don't like that!" to help him express his anger. Simply learning to say "I'm mad" will help him diffuse his anger.

Role-play. Use role-playing to teach your toddler to use words instead of actions in anger-producing situations. For example, have him pretend the TV blanked out during his favorite show or he wasn't able to have a new toy. Using puppets or stuffed animals can make it fun, too.

Run it off. Take your toddler outside and let him burn off that excess energy by running around the yard, climbing play structures, and hollering a little.

Explore art. Give your toddler art materials, such as paper and markers or paint, and suggest he make a "mad" picture. Or if an angry situation occurred, you might say, "Make a picture that shows how you felt when Anthony pushed you down."

Do a dance. Turn on some lively, loud music and let your toddler dance to show his angry feelings. Switch to slow, softer music to help him wind down.

Take a time-out. After an angry outburst or temper tantrum, give your angry toddler a chance to pull himself together, collect his emotions and thoughts, and start fresh after a little time away from the situation or problem.

Love. Tell your child you love him even though he's angry. Reassure him you'll always be there for him.

310. Quick Tip: Let It Out

I think toddlers should have the opportunity to release their pent-up emotions in an appropriate way. I was allowed to get mad by yelling and stomping my feet (but no hitting or kicking) when I was a kid. Encourage your child to express anger in some way—I think it's healthier than keeping it stuffed inside.

—Susan W.

311. Understanding Tantrums

A temper tantrum is the ultimate expression of an overload of emotion. A typical tantrum involves a child throwing himself on the floor while kicking, screaming, crying, flailing his arms, writhing his body, and sometimes holding his breath. The drama and intensity of the behavior may frighten, anger, and embarrass a parent. Here are some tips that will help you understand what's going on when your toddler has a temper tantrum.

Not dangerous. Temper tantrums are rarely dangerous to your child and usually not a sign of any serious emotional disorder. Breath-holding may cause the child to turn blue or faint for a second or two (the child's normal breathing resumes as soon as he faints, and he will recover quickly and completely).

Not your fault. You may wonder what you've done wrong as a parent when your toddler displays such extreme behavior. Be assured, though, a tantrum is simply an outpouring of excess emotion that comes from within—you are not responsible for these episodes.

Common. Almost all young children have at least one tantrum, usually starting around age two or three and tapering off around age four or five.

Creative outlets. Teach your child how to share his feelings through make-believe play or arts and crafts. If he's not able to use words to express his feelings, give him creative alternatives so he won't have to express himself violently.

Product of frustration and anger. A toddler increasingly wants control of his surroundings and the people in them. He continually strives to be independent—often to an extent that is beyond his skill level. He wants results now, and when he struggles with tasks, is thwarted in his efforts, or is denied something he desires, he quickly becomes frustrated and angry. Those two emotions can easily spiral out of control, as he has little experience verbalizing them or expressing them in other ways.

An energy release. Tantrums exhaust the child who is having them. His emotional energy drains out completely during the episode, and he sometimes falls asleep soon afterward.

Frequency. Studies show that toddlers who are anxious or temperamental, who get little rest, who are weak or often ill, or who live in stressful households tend to have tantrums more frequently.

312. Dealing with Tantrums

When your toddler reaches a frustration level that causes him to throw a temper tantrum, try some of the following techniques to help him calm down.

Give him attention ahead of time. A tantrum is an extreme way of getting attention. You can often prevent a tantrum by giving your child the attention he needs when you see a meltdown coming.

Stay calm. Try not to overreact to your toddler's tantrum. Doing so may reinforce the behavior.

Hold your child. Hold him tightly. Physical comfort helps some (but not all) children calm down.

Ignore him. Often it's best to ignore the tantrum. Reprimanding, chastising, or trying to reason with him often backfires. When he settles down on his own, talk about what made him upset.

Talk about frustration. From time to time, talk with your toddler about his feelings to help him learn how to express them.

Act swiftly in public. If your toddler has a tantrum in public and you are uncomfortable or embarrassed, take him away quickly without comment or fuss. Return only after he has calmed down. If leaving is not possible, you may have to restrain him and wait out the tantrum.

313. Dealing with Fear

As your toddler's imagination develops, so do his fears. The world is a magical place for toddlers, and everything seems scary at times—teddy bears, clowns, shadowy furniture, even imaginary monsters under the bed. (See Tip 73.) Here are some tips for helping him deal with scary stuff.

Understand and empathize. Try to understand how your child feels and respect that his fears are real. Never ridicule him for feeling the way he does.

Comfort and reassure. Reassure your toddler by giving him comfort and compassion when he is scared. Hold him and let him know he's safe and that you'll always protect him.

Talk and share. Help him talk about feeling afraid and share some of the fears you felt when you were a child. Talking about fears sometimes helps dispel them.

Model courage. Show your child that you're not afraid in appropriate situations, and he'll learn to be brave by seeing your actions.

Read. Find books that deal with common childhood fears, and read them to your child to show him how other children deal with their fears.

Avoid scaring your child. Don't deliberately scare your child and never force him to face his fears. Scaring him may set him on edge for a long time, and forcing him to face his fears may make them worse.

314. Fear of Strangers

Ironically, at the same time your toddler begins to enjoy his independence, he may also experience a fear of strangers. As he becomes more aware of people he's not familiar with, he may avoid them or cry when they come near him. Such a fear is a normal part of a toddler's emotional development. Here are some tips for minimizing your toddler's fear of strangers.

Prepare for sitters. If you're leaving your toddler with a new babysitter or caregiver, give your child a chance to get acquainted with the person first. Have the sitter over to play for a short time before you leave, or have her visit a few times so the two can get to know each other.

Prepare for visitors. When relatives and friends visit, prepare your toddler by explaining who's coming and what's going to happen. If a visitor wants to approach your toddler or hold him, ask her to be patient and allow your toddler to warm up at his own pace. Avoid using the word *shy* so you don't label your child. Tell the visitor not to take anything personally, that it's his normal behavior toward unfamiliar people.

Help with transitions. Talk to your child about a visitor as she approaches, explaining who she is and why she's there. Quietly suggest to the visitor that she talk with your toddler gently or offer him a toy or other distraction to ease the transition.

Don't force it. Never force your toddler to talk to a stranger, so that he learns to trust his instincts and learns to trust that you'll protect him.

Monitor fears. Sometimes your toddler may fear a familiar person if that person changes his or her appearance in some way. People wearing glasses, beards, hats, costumes, or masks may frighten him. He may also fear men in general, people with loud voices, people in costumes, or even Santa Claus. Talk to your child about the person's appearance and explain that it's normal, but don't force him to make contact with the person.

315. Quick Tip: It's Daddy!

One of my earliest memories is of the time my dad shaved his beard when I was two. He had had the beard since I was born, so I had never known him without it. I remember not wanting to go near him, even though he and my mom kept reassuring me, "It's Daddy, honey. It's okay." I was confused because Daddy had a beard and the stranger sitting in Daddy's spot at our kitchen table didn't. It took me a few hours before I recognized that it really was him.
–Lin L.

316. Mixed Emotions: Sibling Rivalry

If you're bringing home a new baby, your toddler will likely have mixed emotions. Here are some tips to help minimize sibling rivalry at the onset and as the baby grows older.

Prepare. Before the birth, help your toddler understand what life will be like when the baby comes. Let him know that he'll be the "big kid" in the family and that he'll get to do things the baby can't do yet. Read books about new babies, take classes for siblings, and let your toddler help prepare the baby's room.

Understand mixed emotions. Your toddler may feel excited and positive about the new baby, but he may also feel ignored, confused, sad, jealous, resentful, angry, or abandoned. After a few weeks, he may feel disappointed that the new baby cries and sleeps a lot and cannot even play with him.

Give presents. When people come to visit, they often bring a gift for the baby but forget about the older child. If this happens, have a small present (from the new baby!) ready for your toddler.

Make time. Make sure to spend some special time, just you and your toddler, after the baby arrives. Take him to lunch or a movie, play a game or do an activity, or take a walk around the block and talk about his interests and concerns.

Watch. As much as he may profess to "love" the baby, he may harbor negative feelings he's not aware of, or he may handle the baby too roughly. Try not to hover when you let your toddler help out, but keep a watchful eye to prevent problems.

Teach. Show your toddler that the baby cannot hold up his head, grasp a toy, feed himself, or even roll over. Help your toddler see how much the baby needs from others.

Ask for assistance. Ask your toddler to help you figure out what the baby needs. Does he need milk, a diaper change, more blankets, sleep, a change of position, a song, something bright to look at? As your toddler learns the baby's needs and various cues, he may soon be proud of his suggestions and develop a protective feeling toward the baby.

Be careful. As the baby grows older, be careful not to put too much responsibility on your toddler. Remember he's still a little boy with little-boy needs.

Prevent or minimize problems. Before the growing baby can grab your toddler's toys and push over his tower of blocks, try some damage control. Explain how your toddler will soon need to share some of his toys with the baby, but that he can select some of his favorite ones and keep them in a special area.

Let them work it out. As your toddler and the older baby have inevitable squabbles, step back. Often they can work it out themselves within a few minutes.

317. Quick Tip: One-on-One

When I was pregnant with my second child, I worried that my three-year-old would feel left out and jealous. So once a week after the baby was born, I got a sitter for her and took my son out for a special day. We'd go to lunch or the park or a matinee—whatever he wanted to do. We'd talk about his interests, and I'd just devote those two or three hours to his thoughts and needs. I kept it up until he went to kindergarten. It was a very special time for us.

—Lauren R.

318. Encouraging Empathy

As your toddler's sense of self emerges, he has difficulty seeing things from other people's perspectives. Child psychologist Jean Piaget called this orientation "egocentrism." At some point after he learns about his own emotions, he will see that other people have feelings, too. Here's how you can encourage your child's sensitivity and kindness to others.

Model kindness. Listen to your toddler, honor him, protect him, and meet his needs. Be kind and generous to other people and respect their feelings and opinions.

Receive and reinforce. Your toddler will give you more hugs and kisses when he realizes it makes you happy. Reinforce him when he does so by thanking him, smiling, and saying how good you feel.

Watch and praise. Notice how your toddler develops emotional responses to others. He may look worried when a baby or small child cries. If he thinks you are sad, he may look at you intently and want to know why. You may see him pat the head or arm of a younger child who has hurt himself. As you see your toddler reaching out to others, be sure to praise him. This will let him know empathetic actions are valued and appreciated.

Talk about feelings. Ask your child how he would feel if his friends didn't share their toys with him. Ask him how the other children might feel if he didn't share his toys. Tell him how you share your things with others and how you enjoy making others happy.

319. Stepping out Socially

During the toddler's years, your child will develop skills that will allow him to interact with others in a socially acceptable way. Here are some ideas to help you support your toddler's social development.

Personal traits. Your toddler's emerging personality and temperament will play a key role in how he develops socially. He may be, for example, naturally shy (most toddlers are), easygoing, self-confident, or aggressive. Whatever his traits are at the moment, he'll need guidance and modeling to help him learn how to interact effectively with others.

Pace. Take cues from your toddler about how much socializing to do. Generally, you'll want to proceed slowly, starting at home. Focus on sharing, being cooperative, taking turns, being a leader and being a follower, and helping others.

Imitation. One of the primary ways toddlers learn social skills is through imitation. When your child watches your social behavior, he'll learn sensible social rules. When he watches his peers, however, he may see a lot of grabbing, hitting, biting, name-calling, and other inappropriate behavior. Close supervision will be necessary when your toddler interacts with any group of children.

Social opportunities. When your toddler has one or two friends over, it's a great opportunity for him to learn important social skills such as sharing and taking turns. (See Tip 174.) Emotions may run high at first, as your toddler copes with sharing beloved toys and, perhaps for the first time, sharing the spotlight. Other helpful social outings include having dinner with another family, visiting neighbors, playing at a playground, and attending children's events with relatives or friends.

Media influences. Although not as powerful as parents, the characters in books, videos, and TV do provide social modeling that a toddler may imitate. Be sure to monitor the quality of the media that influences your child.

Feedback. When your child interacts with others, your feedback about his social skills will be important. He needs your encouragement when he's doing fine as well as your guidance when he could improve.

Manners. Be sure to use and teach good manners to your child, as they are a big part of social development. Say "please," "thank you," "you're welcome," "excuse me," and so on. Model and teach manners such as waiting until someone has finished speaking, modulating your voice in libraries and other public places, and waiting for your turn.

320. Quick Tip: Greetings and Good-byes

I found a good way to teach my toddler about gracious hellos and good-byes. I'd simply take him with me when I answered the door to greet people and when I walked guests to the door for good-byes. I didn't expect him to participate (although sometimes he did), but I knew he would gradually pick up these social skills just by hearing me do it so often.

—Ricardo A.

321. Quick Tip: Not Quite Ready

Sometimes a young child isn't ready to socialize with more than one friend at a time. I had this problem with my daughter. She became very possessive and very irritable when several children came to play or when I babysat other kids. I learned to introduce her to one child at a time, and she did much better.

—Rosa R.

322. Preschool

Sometime after age two your toddler may be ready to attend preschool. Most preschools don't take children until they're two and a half and potty trained, but others are more flexible. Here are some tips for determining if your toddler is ready and how to prepare him.

Friends. Does your toddler like to play with friends? If so, he may be ready for preschool and all the new friends he'll make there. Have a few friends over and watch how he gets along with others.

Independence. Does your toddler like to do things himself? If so, he may enjoy the feeling of independence he gains by going to preschool by himself. Watch for signs of autonomy, such as dressing himself.

Social skills. Does your child share his toys with others? Does he understand how to take turns? If so, he'll get a chance to use and enhance his social skills at preschool. Work on sharing and taking turns at home before sending him to school.

Gradual transition. Does your toddler have a long attention span? Does he have enough energy to play for a couple of hours, or does he get tired quickly? Maybe try a couple short sessions a week until he's ready for longer and more frequent sessions.

323. Quick Tip:
Prepare through Play

Before your toddler goes to preschool, give him lots of play dates with friends so he's used to interacting with other kids. It makes the transition easier if your child has already developed some social skills.

—Dana M.

324. Quick Tip:
Choosing a Preschool

I decided to send my daughter to preschool instead of day-care when I thought she was ready to socialize more with other kids. The children were all her age. The teachers were credentialed and experienced and knew how to work with kids. And I felt having a preschool experience would make it easier when it came time for her to go to kindergarten. She loved preschool, made lots of friends, and really made gains in her social and language skills.

—Dana M.

325. Quick Tip: Transition Object

When your toddler goes off to preschool, he may have trouble separating from you. My son did. The preschool teacher told me to send along a transitional object—something familiar and special like a blanket or stuffed animal. I let my son decide what to take. He chose his teddy bear and put it in his cubby at school. It seemed to make him feel more secure.

—Orlando T.

326. Quick Tip: First Day

I bought my son a new lunch box and a backpack for his first day of preschool. I also played his favorite CD of children's songs while we drove in the car. On the way to school I asked him what he wanted to do when he got there, and on the way home he told me what he'd done. It was a great experience for him.

—Susan W.

Chapter 16
Childcare

327. Work In or Out of the Home?

If you've stayed home with your child since she was a baby, you may consider returning to work outside the home now that she's a toddler. This is a difficult decision for anyone to make and there are many factors to weigh. The first factor is how you feel about working in or out of the home. Here are some questions to ponder.

- Do you enjoy staying home with your child? Do you enjoy your career outside the home?
- Does your career outside the home provide a good income?
- Is staying home with your child rewarding? Is working outside the home rewarding?
- What are the benefits of staying home or returning to your career?
- How much would childcare cost, compared to the income of your job outside the home? (See Tip 329.)
- Do you want to return to your job outside the home? Do you want to stay at home with your child?
- What other options do you have when it comes to working and childcare?
- Who do you want caring for your child?

328. Quick Tip: Going Back

When my son was born, I quit my job to be a stay-at-home mom. It was a great decision for me and my family. When my son was three, though, I started to think about going back to work. I loved being with my son, but I also missed the rewards—financial and otherwise—my career offered. After weighing all my options and the pros and cons, I decided to return to work. It took me some time to adjust to the new situation, and it took my son some time to adjust to childcare. Nevertheless, this has proven to be another great decision for me and my family.

—Lin L.

329. Coping with the Cost

If you're thinking about going back to work, you may want to make up a profit-and-loss sheet to see if your salary will cover the cost of childcare—and whether it's worth going back to work. Here are some points to consider.

Compare income to expenses. From your after-tax income, deduct all of your regular expenses and then deduct any new expenses involved in returning to work, such as new clothing, transportation, lunches, and so on. If applicable, decide whether health insurance provided by an employer would cost more or less than what you pay for a private policy. Then compare your adjusted income (what's left after your expenses) to the cost of your childcare. If there's not a great difference, you might find it more economical to stay home.

Work part-time. As a compromise, find out if working part-time would be feasible financially. Or depending on your type of work, see if your employer will allow you to work a certain percentage of your full-time hours from home, which would decrease your childcare costs.

Start a home business. Consider starting a home business, such as daycare, computer work, or telephone sales. You could make money while being at home with your toddler.

Check preschools and childcare discounts. Try to find a preschool that will also serve as your childcare, which may save you some money. Ask prospective childcare facilities if they offer discounts when you help out or contribute your time in some way.

Bring her to work. If your workplace is kid-friendly and kid-safe, ask if you can bring your child a couple of days a week.

Cut down on expenses. Think about ways you can cut down on your regular expenses so you can afford to stay home with your toddler. You might consider getting rid of cable TV, cell phones, dinners out, movie rentals, and so on in an effort to save money.

330. Quick Tip: Do the Math

I dreaded going back to work and wondered how I was going to leave my son. But I felt guilty not contributing to the household income. So I sat down and did the math, and figured out my take-home salary would be almost equal to the cost of daycare. I decided to cut out a few luxuries and spend the time with my son at home. I've never regretted it.

—Kathi A.

331. Finding Providers

If you decide to go back to work, you'll need to find appropriate childcare for your toddler. Here are some tips to consider when starting your search.

Childcare options. Many childcare options may be available to you. These include your partner, a close relative, a licensed home daycare provider, a commercial daycare center, on-site daycare offered by an employer, a babysitter, a nanny, or a parent co-op.

Getting referrals. In addition to asking friends, neighbors, and relatives for childcare referrals, look to the greater community for help. Contact the local hospital or ask your pediatrician for a list of people who offer childcare. The fire or police department, Red Cross, or local recreation centers sometimes offer babysitting classes and keep lists of graduates. A child development department at a local college may have a list of students who offer childcare. You can also check for referrals from your local social service agency.

332. Quick Tip: Two-Parent Job

My husband wasn't very involved in finding childcare for our son. He seemed to think the "problem" was mine. But when I pointed out that our son belonged to both of us and how important it was to find the right place for him, he finally got the picture. Once he started, he really got into it—and that was a great help.

—Jennifer R.

333. Checklist for Safety

When your toddler goes to a home or commercial site for childcare, you'll want to make sure the setting is safe. Licensed childcare providers are required to keep their sites clean and safe, and they are checked regularly. But they may overlook something that's important to you. Here are some safety tips to check for.

- Is the site licensed or registered?
- Has the site been inspected lately?
- Have there been any infractions in the safety check?
- Is there a reasonable ratio of caregivers to children?
- Is the area clean, including the bathrooms and kitchen?
- Are the toys and materials safe, clean, and appropriate for your child's age?
- Are there operational smoke detectors, fire alarms, and sprinklers at the site?
- Is there an easy escape route for the children in case of an emergency?
- Is the outdoor area enclosed and safe for kids?
- Is the place toddler-proofed, with covered outlets, no open cords, gated stairs, and so on?
- Is the site well ventilated with fresh air?
- Are chemical products and hazardous materials put away?
- Is the garbage inaccessible?
- Is the food fresh, clean, and safe for toddlers?
- Is the site adequately spacious and well furnished with play equipment and other relevant materials?

334. Guarding against Abuse

Unfortunately, finding a trustworthy caregiver who will not emotionally or physically abuse your toddler is a major concern today. If family, friends, or neighbors are not options for you, you may have to leave your child with a virtual stranger, which may cause anxiety. Here are some tips to help you find a responsible caregiver.

Ask the caregiver's clients. One of the best ways to research a caregiver is to ask her clients—parents with children at that daycare site—if they've had any problems or misgivings with the provider.

Contact the caregiver's references. Call the references and ask them about the caregiver's trustworthiness.

Make sure the caregiver is licensed. Licensed caregivers are checked routinely by state agencies to ensure their sites are safe and clean.

Research. Check with your city, county, or state social services agencies to see if any negative reports about the caregiver are on file.

Request an observational visit. Ask the caregiver if you can come over and watch her in action. She shouldn't have any qualms about letting you observe her.

Drop by. Drop by, rather than call ahead, for your initial meeting. Observe how the children are doing when the caregiver doesn't expect you. Likewise, after choosing a caregiver, stop by occasionally or come early to pick up your toddler so you can see how things are going.

Ask your child. Kids are smart and have a good sense about people. Ask your child if she likes the caregiver and why or why not.

Trust your instincts. Find another caregiver if you have any concerns at all.

335. Quick Tip: Happy Kid, Caring Caregiver

My biggest fear was finding a good caregiver after hearing horror stories about abusive ones. But I soon knew my son was in good hands because he had a big smile on his face whenever he saw his caregiver. I don't think he would have been so happy if she hadn't been a caring person.

—Ann P.

336. Interviewing the Caregiver

When looking for childcare, you'll want to interview several providers. This is a chance to discuss issues such as parenting philosophy, discipline, nutrition, naptime, and so on and to learn more about the caregiver. Ultimately, trust your gut if you sense something isn't right during the interview.

Ask pertinent questions. In addition to discussing the issues important to you, ask specific questions, such as the following.

- What is your background with children?
- Why do you want to work with kids?
- What are your credentials? Have you taken any child development classes?
- Do you have any references I may contact?
- What are your time constraints?
- How do you handle situations such as illness and discipline?
- How will you transport my toddler, if necessary? Do you use seatbelts? Do you have any driving violations in the last five years?
- How is your overall health? Do you smoke? Drink? Take any medications or drugs?

What's your impression? After you've interviewed the person, think about your overall impression of her.

- Did the person communicate well?
- Was the person neatly dressed and clean?
- Did the person greet you or arrive on time?
- Did the person have a pleasing personality?
- Did the person seem comfortable being interviewed?
- If your child met the person, how did she react to her?
- Was there anything about the person that bothered you?

337. Quick Tip: Peace of Mind

I interviewed about ten childcare providers. I just wasn't about to leave my son with someone I wasn't completely comfortable with. Yes, it took a couple of weeks to find the right one, but it was worth my peace of mind.
—Colleen C.

338. Babysitter Tips

If you decide to use a babysitter for childcare, here are some tips for making the arrangement as smooth as possible.

Choose the familiar. If possible, find a sitter your toddler knows well and feels comfortable with, such as a grandparent, aunt, or neighbor. Sitters who love your child are likely to do a great job caring for her.

Use available resources. Friends and family can often recommend a good sitter. Your local church, recreation center, or high school may also provide referrals. Many organizations put on instructional classes for babysitters. You may want to offer to pay for such a class if you want her to be well prepared.

Prepare your child. Talk to your toddler about why the sitter is coming, what she will be doing, and where you're going. Offer as much information as you can to help your child understand the situation. Answer her questions as honestly as you can.

Use doll play. While you're at home with your child, have her make-believe she's babysitting her doll or teddy bear. Show your child how to take care of the doll while Mommy and Daddy are out.

Make the first time short and sweet. If your toddler isn't used to having a sitter, make the first experience short so she has a chance to ease into the situation. Have the sitter come early so you can observe how she interacts with your child.

Promote fun time. Buy a new game or toy for your toddler to share with the babysitter, so she's entertained and preoccupied while you're gone.

Provide emergency information. Show your sitter the list of phone numbers you keep in the event of an emergency (see Tip 130), such as 911, your doctor, poison control, relatives, and neighbors. Also give her the number to your cell phone and the place where you'll be. If your child has any allergies or other problems, alert the sitter so she's well prepared to deal the situation.

339. Quick Tip: Know Your Sitter

I always used babysitters who were recommended by people I knew and respected. The first few times a sitter came, I stayed around the house and watched how she interacted with my child. For me, that was the best way to be convinced that the person would work out.

—Tiffany G

340. Quick Tip: Don't Dawdle

Invite your sitter to come early and play with your toddler before you need to leave. When it's time to go, make sure to reassure your child that everything will be okay, and tell him when you'll be home. But don't stick around forever, dragging things out. A slow good-bye just makes things harder for everyone.

—Dana M.

341. Babysitting Co-ops

Establishing or joining a babysitting co-op is a great way to save money on sitters, build a network of friends for your child, and get to know other parents with children the same age as yours. Here are some tips to keep in mind.

The basics. A babysitting co-op allows parents to take care of one another's children, earn credits for sitting, and spend the credits when they need a sitter. Members can use the co-op as much or as little as they like.

Meeting the group. Have a meeting with all the parents to get to know one another and to determine the rules of the co-op. Put a limit on the number of kids members can watch at one time, decide on a system to keep track of how many hours members use and owe, agree on safety precautions, choose a coordinator, and so on. Then have occasional meetings to discuss problems and concerns, new members, changes, and so on.

Safety considerations. Make sure all the parents have toddler-proofed their homes. Have the group coordinator visit each home to check for safety concerns.

Problems. If you have problems with a member, discuss the situation at a meeting and try to resolve it. If a problem persists, you may have to ask participants to leave the group.

342. Easing Separation Anxiety

Many toddlers have first-day jitters when they go to childcare. Until they're comfortable with the new surroundings and new caregiver, they may be anxious, fearful, and upset. Here are some tips to help with separation anxiety.

Prepare your child ahead of time. Explain in simple terms why you need to be away and how the caregiver will help her. Tell your toddler some details about the caregiver and what the environment and experience will be like. Answer her questions as fully as you can, so she begins to understand the situation.

Pay a visit or two before starting. Let your child get to know the caregiver while you're there, and explore the setting together so she knows what to expect.

Let her take something special. Your child will feel safer if she has something from home, such as a blanket, a stuffed animal, or a favorite object. (See Tip 325.)

Get her going. Help your toddler find something fun to do when she arrives, so she's involved when you leave. She'll be less likely to get upset if she's busy.

Say good-bye. Be sure to tell your child you're leaving. Don't sneak out, trying to avoid a scene. She'll lose trust in you if you're not open about leaving.

Invite a friend over. After your toddler has met a friend, see if the friend can come and play one day. That way your child may look forward to seeing her friend at childcare.

343. The Parent-Caregiver Bond

Your toddler will sense your feelings toward your caregiver, which may affect how she accepts the person. Here are some tips to foster your relationship with your caregiver.

Show interest. Ask your caregiver how she's enjoying the job, ask her about her day, and so on. Let her know you're interested in her as an individual and not just as the person who watches your child.

Be thoughtful. Don't forget to say thank you to the caregiver when you pick up your child. Compliment her if she does something special for your child, such as take her for a walk to the park or make a fun snack. Bring her a small gift on her birthday or other occasion to let her know you're happy with her care of your child.

Keep communication open. Tell her to feel free to talk about anything having to do with the job, and then really listen to her when she approaches you with something. If there's a problem, try to work out a solution that satisfies both of you.

Understand your feelings. Be prepared. You might experience a little jealousy if your child shows affection toward the caregiver or is reluctant to leave at the end of the day. But her actions are a good sign—you want your child to be happy with her caregiver. Remember, there's no replacing a parent, no matter what delightful person comes along.

344. Quick Tip: From One Good Thing to Another

At first I was really jealous that my daughter latched onto her caregiver so quickly. I mean, she really seemed to love the woman. When my daughter didn't want to leave, I thought the caregiver was taking my place. Then I realized she was just so comfortable and having so much fun that she didn't want to leave. I started telling her what I had planned for her when we left, and that made the transition easier.

—Stephanie C.

345. Sharing Childcare Duties with Your Partner

Handling childcare is the responsibility of both parents, not just one. If you both work full-time, you may have very limited time to find the right childcare provider, get your toddler to and from the site, work out schedules, and so on. Here are some tips to help the two of you handle childcare as a team.

Common goals. Talk about what you want for childcare so you're both on the same page. Doing so will help you avoid miscommunication about the details.

Location, location, location. If possible, find a site that works for both of you, so you can share dropping off and picking up your child without being late to work or going out of your way.

Driving schedule. Work out a driving schedule based on your time constraints and the locations of your jobs and the childcare site. Perhaps one of you could take your toddler to the site, while the other one picks her up at the end of the day.

Sick days. If your child is sick and can't go to childcare, take turns staying home with her. If one of you can't afford the time off, take turns covering for each other, and make up the days another time.

Compromise. If it's impossible for one parent to drive to and from daycare, work out a compromise. For example, that parent could pick up some of the other parent's tasks, such as mowing the lawn, running errands, grocery shopping, preparing meals, shoveling snow, taking out the garbage and recycling, keeping the cars washed and filled with gas, balancing checkbooks, cleaning the garage, and so on.

Talk about it. If you have a concern about the childcare situation, talk about it with your partner. Discuss the problem and see if you can work out a positive solution together.

The ultimate sharing. While few couples can swing it, some avoid the need for childcare by finding flexible jobs so one of them is always home with their toddler. Sometimes this entails one or both partners working less than forty hours per week.

346. When Your Toddler Is Ill

Everything is going smoothly with childcare—and then your toddler gets ill. Here are some tips to help you cope with the situation.

Kids are going to get sick. One of the drawbacks of daycare is that your toddler will pick up more viruses and germs. But the benefits of childcare usually outweigh the inconvenience of colds and sore throats. Accept it as part of your toddler's life.

Check with your childcare provider. Some providers don't find a sick child a problem or have provisions for sick kids, such as a special room or special policies. Many providers recognize that by the time a child's symptoms are apparent, the illness has already spread.

Determine how sick your toddler is. If your child is vomiting or has diarrhea, a fever or sore throat, an eye or ear infection, a rash, severe pain, trouble breathing, or a contagious disease, call your doctor for advice or treatment. Keep your toddler home until the doctor says it's safe for her to return to daycare.

Stay home. If your child is sick and you feel she needs your care, then take the day off. Some companies allow employees to use sick days when they need to stay home with a sick child. Often a day of rest and pampering are enough to get your toddler back on her feet.

Check into alternative childcare centers. Some childcare sites take sick kids on an emergency basis. You may be able to find a substitute facility when you can't take your toddler to her regular daycare and when you can't stay home with her.

Home care. See if you can find a childcare provider who is willing to come to your home when you can't leave work. Or find a temporary nurse for the day, if necessary.

347. Quick Tip: Save the Days

When I returned to work after I had a baby, I started hoarding my sick and vacation days. I saved them to use when my toddler got sick. It was worth the sacrifice to know I could stay home with him when he needed me.
                                                                    —Tracy O.

348. Childcare: When It's Time to Make a Change

There may come a time when you need to make a change in your childcare situation. Perhaps the childcare provider just isn't working out, your child is unhappy there, or the provider is retiring or taking a vacation. Here are some tips to make the transition to a new caregiver.

Talk about the change. Don't bring up the subject too soon, but do talk about it a few days before the change, so your toddler is somewhat prepared.

Chat with the caregiver. Have your childcare provider talk to your toddler about the change, too. That way she can tell your child she still cares for her, even though there will be a change.

Visit the new site. The same way you eased your toddler into the first childcare situation, give your toddler a chance to become acquainted with the new caregiver and site before she makes the change. (See Tip 342.)

Bring a lovey. Let your toddler bring along a lovey or something special to make her feel secure with the change.

Give your child time. Your toddler may take a little time to adjust to the new situation, so be patient. She may ask about the previous caregiver and may not understand what's happened. Answer her questions simply, reassure her, and talk about her new situation.

Don't hesitate to move on. If you find that your toddler is really unhappy at her new childcare, look into it. There may be another problem, and you may want to look for another caregiver. You may feel frustrated by the "revolving childcare" game, but finding a caregiver you and your child can trust is worth every effort.

349. Quick Tip: Make It Concrete

When my daughter's caregiver went on vacation and we had to find a new provider for a few weeks, she just didn't understand. She kept asking and asking for her old caregiver. Finally I showed her pictures of our last vacation to help her make the connection. We talked about what her caregiver was probably doing on her vacation, and how many days it would be until she came back. Making it concrete for my daughter helped her understand.
—Charles F.

Chapter 17
Traveling

350. Car Safety Seats for Toddlers

Even though most people know the dangers of driving without a car safety seat for their babies and toddlers, more children are killed as passengers in car crashes than from any other injury. Part of the problem is the incorrect use of a car safety seat. Always use a government-approved car safety seat that's properly installed using the directions that come with the car seat. Your toddler's life may depend on it. Here are some tips to make sure your toddler is secure in his car safety seat.

Before buying, check for the right fit. Choose a car safety seat that is made for your child's size and weight. When buying a seat, put your child in it, adjust the harnesses and buckles, and check to make sure the fit works well for him. Then make sure the seat fits in your car before you buy it.

Before buying, check the model for safety. Before you buy a new car safety seat or install a used one, check with the Consumer Product Safety Commission (www.cpsc.gov) to make sure the seat is a safe one.

Follow manufacturers instructions. Read the instructions on the car safety seat and keep them handy in the glove compartment for future reference. Also, read your car manual for tips on how to install the car safety seat correctly. Use the harnesses correctly and make sure they're snug.

Put the car safety seat in the back seat. *Always* place your toddler's car safety seat in the backseat. In the event of an accident, a deployed air bag can seriously injure your toddler—especially if he's in a rear-facing safety seat.

Booster seats. Keep your child in a car safety seat as long as you can. When he finally outgrows it, use a booster seat and make sure your car seat belts fit him snugly across the chest and thighs. Do not sling belts across his neck or stomach.

Caution. Do not use a car safety seat that is more than ten years old, does not have a date of manufacture on it, does not have a model number, does not come with instructions, has cracks, was ever in a car crash, or is missing any parts.

Never leave your child unattended in the car.

351. Fun in the Car

Traveling with your toddler may become challenging as he develops his own identity and independence. Here are some tips for taking longer trips with your energetic child.

Explain the trip. If you're planning to take a long drive, tell your toddler about the trip, what he'll see along the way, and what you've planned for the ride. Do the same for plane rides or other forms of transportation.

Bring some fun stuff. Fill a travel bag with some old and new toys, books, and whatever security object your toddler uses. Your toddler can enjoy the items while riding in the car. You may want to change the contents each time you take a trip to keep him surprised and interested.

Play music and sing songs. Play some of your toddler's favorite tapes or CDs or sing some songs together. Make up songs about things you see along the way.

Chat. Talk to your toddler while you drive to keep his interest and stimulate his mind. Play word games, and talk about your day, where you're going, and what your plans are.

Take breaks. Make frequent stops along the way for snacks, diaper or bathroom breaks, sightseeing, and so on. Be sure to breathe in lots of fresh air and stretch, walk, or even run a little. If your toddler gets upset during a long trip, take a break and comfort him.

Offer special treats. While on your trip, buy your toddler a small treat or inexpensive souvenir to thank him for good behavior and to keep him occupied.

Enjoy snack time. Bring along sippy cups of water and finger food packed in easy-to-open containers so your toddler can help himself. Have napkins and wet wipes for easy cleanup.

352. Quick Tip: Toy Time

My daughter was really wiggly in her car seat. She hated it and squirmed and cried when she was in it. I brought along a bucket of toys and set them in the front seat where she couldn't see them. Then every time she'd start fussing, I'd pass a toy back to her. That would keep her entertained at least for a few blocks. Eventually she learned to associate car seat time with toy time.

—Kris N.

353. Quick Tip: Rotate the Fun

I always rotated the playthings in the car from time to time to keep them fresh and interesting for my kids. I also had one bag of goodies for them to play with in the car, and another bag to take into restaurants. Shifting the toys around made them seem new, which kept my kids happier for longer periods of time.

—Anne G.

354. Quick Tip: Keep an Eye Out

Before we left on a long car ride, I'd cut out magazine pictures of things I thought we might see along way, such as a McDonald's sign, a dog, a fire truck, a bridge, and so on. I glued the pictures to a sheet of construction paper and covered it with clear Contact paper. Then I gave my daughter the sheet and some happy-face stickers and told her to put a sticker on a picture whenever she found the item. She had a great time finding the objects.

—Robin B.

355. Air Travel

When you're planning a trip that includes an airline flight, you'll need to make special accommodations for your toddler. Here are some suggestions to help you prepare.

Call the airlines. Ask what they have to offer a traveling toddler, such as special seating, special foods, and so on.

Travel during sleep time. Airplane travel often induces sleep in children, so if possible schedule the flight around your toddler's naptime or bedtime.

Go nonstop. If you don't have to change planes on the trip, your child won't have to be disturbed and won't have to endure the long lines and waiting that are usually involved.

Bring activities. Fill a small backpack with a variety of things for your toddler to do on the trip—for example, coloring books and crayons, stickers, picture books, audiotapes, puzzles, and games.

Dress comfortably. Let your toddler wear pajamas or loose-fitting sweats that can be removed if the plane is warm. Bring an extra sweater in case the plane is cold.

Protect his ears. If your child has a cold or ear infection, give him an age-appropriate dose of a cold or pain-relieving medication before the flight. On takeoff and landing, have him chew on a soft candy or drink through a straw to cause him to swallow.

Take breaks. Ask for an aisle seat so you can get out of your seats easily when your toddler needs to use the bathroom.

Don't forget. Pack a carryon with extra diapers, wet wipes, a first-aid kit, a change of clothes, snacks, and a couple of new toys.

356. Quick Tip: Toddler Boarding

The airlines always give families traveling with children the chance to board early, but for some kids this really isn't a good idea. It just means your child is on the plane longer. I stay close to the boarding area and let my toddler walk around, getting out some of his energy. After everyone else has boarded and the plane is close to takeoff, I take him on the plane so we don't have to wait long.

—Orlando T.

357. Quick Tip: Puppet Play

I always brought puppets to entertain my toddler when we traveled on airplanes and stayed in motels or hotels. For some reason, he thought the puppet play seemed extra fun in these situations.

—Dana M.

358. Camping with Your Toddler

Camping with a toddler can be a challenge, but if you plan ahead, stay relaxed, and keep an eye on your child, the experience can be a great adventure for all of you. Here are some tips for camping with your toddler.

Prepare for the trip. Make lists, including one with everything you think your toddler will need on the trip.

Think about safety. You'll want to protect your toddler from outdoor hazards, including poisonous plants, bug bites, sunburn, unfriendly animals, severe weather, and unsafe terrain. (See Chapter 9.)

Pack food and drink. Make sure you have a good supply of your toddler's favorite foods and plenty of liquids.

Bring first aid. Take along a first-aid kit (see Tip 137), and think about adding a few extra items that might be needed on the trip—for example, kid-safe insect repellent, sunburn medication, and so on.

Prepare for fears. Since you'll be staying in a strange environment, prepare your toddler for the camping experience. Tell him about what he can expect there, where you'll be sleeping, and that you'll keep him safe.

Light up, if needed. Give your toddler his own flashlight, in case he becomes afraid of the dark.

Don't worry about the dirt. Your toddler is bound to get dirty while camping. Try not to worry about it, let him enjoy the environment, and wash him up at the end of the day (or the trip).

Safety. Keep a constant eye on your toddler. Plan what you would do in case of an emergency.

359. Quick Tip:
It's Worth the Trouble

My husband and I did a lot of camping before our daughter was born, so we didn't think twice about bringing her along when she was old enough to enjoy the experience. Of course, it took a whole lot of extra planning and packing, but it was well worth it. She had a ball. We've been going every year since she was two.

—Susan W.

360. Staying in Hotels

Most kids love staying overnight in hotels or motels, where the big bed is not only for sleeping, but also for playing and a little jumping. Here are tips for taking your toddler to a hotel.

Child-friendly. Choose a hotel that welcomes children. Many hotels offer free meals for kids and have lots of other amenities to offer children, such as a playroom, a kiddy swimming pool, children's videos and video games, cable TV, and snack machines.

Ask for extras. Most hotels provide cribs or extra beds, so take advantage of these offerings. It may be easier than packing your own bedding along for your toddler.

Kitchenette. If possible, choose a hotel with a kitchenette so you can prepare meals or snacks for your toddler. Even a room with a refrigerator can make a difference.

Room service. Don't forget to take advantage of room service if your child is hungry at night and you're out of snacks.

Babysitting. Some hotels offer babysitting so you can go out while your toddler is kept busy with a sitter. Or consider bringing your usual babysitter along if it's a short trip.

Have fun. Treat the hotel stay as a special event and make it fun. Let your toddler help you get ice, buy a drink from the machine, jump on the bed, watch a special TV show, snuggle in bed with you, and explore the grounds under your supervision. Bring along a game to play and some activities to keep your toddler occupied in the room.

361. Quick Tip: Overnighter Vacation

My twins love going to a hotel for an overnight. I think it's because we've got the whole family in one room, and they can have our full attention. They get to watch movies on TV until late at night, order room service, and sleep on foldout couches or rollaways, which they think is a big adventure. When we can't afford to take a real vacation, sometimes we just go to a hotel for a night of family fun.
—Shanice A.

362. International Travel

If you're planning to leave the country with your toddler, there are a few extra things you can do to make the trip easier.

Get passports. If your travel requires passports for your child, be sure to arrange them well ahead of time.

Documentation. When traveling abroad, you may need documentation to prove your child is legally yours.

Medications. If your toddler is on a medication, speak with his doctor and arrange to have enough for the trip. Ask for special medications that might be needed in case your child gets sick.

Foods. If your child has a special diet or doesn't like certain foods, you may want to bring a supply of his favorites on the trip.

363. Quick Tip: Overseas Flight

When we went to Italy with two toddlers, I brought along lots of activities and toys for the long flight. They slept for part of it, but when they were awake, about every half hour I'd bring out something new from my goody bag—paper dolls, felt markers, puppets—inexpensive things that would keep them busy. It made the trip a whole lot easier.

—Connie P.

364. Moving Across Time Zones

Your toddler may get his days and nights mixed up when you're traveling across time zones. Here are some tips to help.

Travel at night. That way, your toddler is likely to sleep most of the time.

Nap or rest right away. When you arrive at your destination, have your toddler nap so he'll be well-rested and refreshed with energy.

Take it easy. If possible, avoid doing too much the first day of your trip so your child has a better chance to adjust to the time zone.

Bed down early. If he seems to need it, put your toddler to bed early the first night and let him sleep in.

Watch for signs. In the early evening, notice when your toddler seems tired, then do your usual bedtime routine. Sing him a song, give him a bath, rock him, read to him, and so on.

Be flexible. If your child isn't sleepy, let him stay awake until he's ready to go to bed or take a nap.

365. Quick Tip: Time Change

I was really worried about how the time change would affect my toddler when we went to Europe. I thought he'd mix up his days and nights and we'd all be miserable. Turned out I had trouble with the time change, but he adapted really well. We just gave him a couple of extra naps, and he caught up quickly.

—Lin L.

Recommended Reading

The Arts and Crafts Busy Book
Trish Kuffner, Meadowbrook Press, 2003.

Baby Birthday Parties
Penny Warner, Meadowbrook Press, 1999.

The Complete Resource Book for Toddlers and Twos
Pam Schiller, Gryphon House, 2003.

Discipline without Shouting or Spanking
Jerry Wyckoff, Ph.D. and Barbara C. Unell,
Meadowbrook Press, 2002.

The Girlfriends' Guide to Toddlers
Vicki Iovine, Perigee, 1999.

Healthy Food for Healthy Kids
Bridget Swinney, M.S., R.D., Meadowbrook Press, 1999.

Parent-Tested Ways to Grow Your Child's Confidence
Silvana Clark, Meadowbrook Press, 2000.

Practical Parenting Tips
Vicki Lansky, Meadowbrook Press, 2003.

Preschooler Play & Learn
Penny Warner, Meadowbrook Press, 1998.

The Preschooler's Busy Book
   Trish Kuffner, Meadowbrook Press, 2003.

Secrets of the Baby Whisperer for Toddlers
   Tracy Hogg, Ballantine Books, 2003.

Strategies for Stay-at-Home Parents
   Kris Berggren, Meadowbrook Press, 2003.

The Toddler's Busy Book
   Trish Kuffner, Meadowbrook Press, 1999.

Toilet Training without Tears or Trauma
   Penny Warner and Paula Kelly, M.D.,
   Meadowbrook Press, 2003.

What to Expect: The Toddler Years
   Arlene Eisenberg, Heidi E. Murkoff,
   and Sandee E. Hathaway, B.S.N.,
   Workman Publishing Company, 1996.

Index

A

Abuse, child, 338

Accidents. *See* Medical emergencies; Safety

Adapter seats, toilet, 104

Air travel, 360–2

Allergies, 6, 14–5

American Academy of Pediatrics, 2, 76

Anger, expressing, 312–3

Animal dance, 214

Animal games, 178

Animals, sorting, 252

Apologizing, 159

Appliances, 143, 145

Armpit thermometer, 79

Arts and crafts
activities for, 226–8
basics for, 224
clay, 229
crayons, learning colors with, 243
displaying projects from, 286
drawing, 222–3
expressing emotions with, 312, 315
materials for, 225
play dough, 229, 230
scribbling, 230–1

Associative play, 169

Authoritarian parenting style, 151

Axillary thermometer, 79

B

Babysitters
co-ops and, 344
at hotels, 365
preparing child for, 318
safety prevention and, 136, 142
using for childcare, 342–3
See also Childcare (providers)

Baby talk, 269

Balls, 187, 194, 212, 217

Band-Aids, 86

Barbecue burns, 203

Bathroom, toddler-proofing, 145

Baths
cleaning tips for, 38
encouraging, 46
play during, 41–3, 45
shampooing in, 38, 40, 43
singing during, 41, 44
toys for, 39–40

Bathtub, toddler-proofing, 145

Bed
family, 56, 57
transition to a big, 58–9

Bedtime
coping with monsters at, 66–7
extending, 68
getting toddler to sleep at, 54–5
keeping toddler in bed at, 64
stalling at, 62–3
stories at, 60–1
See also Sleep

Behavior issues
  biting and hitting, 158–9
  negativity, 162
  positive reinforcement and, 163
  whining, 160–1
  See also Discipline
Bilingual families, 264–5
Birthday parties, 16, 300–2
Birth order, 292–3
Biting, 158–9
Blocks, 186
Board games, 253
Body language, 263
Boo-boos. *See* Injuries
Books. *See* Reading and books
Bottle-feeding
  irritable bowel and, 16
  weaning to cup from, 4–5
Bowel movements
  holding, 119
  terminology for, 103
Boys vs. girls, 290–1
Breastfeeding, 2–3
Bruises, 133
Bubbles, 186
Bunny rabbit method of tying
  shoes, 236
Button sorting, 233

C

Camping, 362–4
Carbohydrates, 7, 8
Caregivers. *See* Babysitters,
  Childcare (providers)

Car seats, 135, 356–7
Car travel, 356–60
Chalking, 196
Changing table, 146
Chapped nose, home remedy
  for, 84
Chemicals, 145
Childcare (providers)
  abuse and, 338–9
  costs and, 334
  illnesses and, 350
  interviewing, 340–1
  parent-caregiver bond and,
    346–7
  safety and, 337
  searching for, 336
  separation anxiety and, 345
  sharing duties with partners
    when handling, 348–9
  transition to a new, 352–3
  See also Babysitters
Child proofing, 140–7
Choices, offering
  baths and, 46
  cognitive skill development
    and, 240
  fostering independence with,
    298
  negativity and, 162
Choking, 129–31
Chores, 286
Clapping, 214
Classification skills
  comparing and contrasting

Estimating, 251
Exercise, 68

F

Family bed, 56, 57
Fat, 7, 9
Fears
  bedtime monsters and, 63, 66–7
  camping and, 363
  doctor visits and, 87, 93
  helping child deal with, 317
  of strangers, 318–9
  of the toilet, 118
Feeding. *See* Breastfeeding;
    Food(s); Mealtime
Fevers, 80–1
Fine motor skills
  arts and crafts activities for,
    226–8
  developing with clay and
    dough, 229–30
  drawing and, 222–3
  dressing and, 234–5
  everyday opportunities for
    developing, 232–3
  gender differences and, 290
  scribbling and, 230–1
  tying shoes and, 236–7
  See also Gross motor skills
Finger foods, 10–2
Finger paints, 187, 227
Finger play, 276–9
Fingers, smashed, 133

First-aid kits, 126, 132
Firstborn characteristics, 292
Flashlights, 64
Fluids. *See* Liquid intake
Fluoride, 47
Flushing the toilet, 114
Follow-the-leader, 196
Food(s)
  allergies to, 14–5
  at birthday parties, 301
  changing appetite and prefer-
    ences for, 12, 13
  children helping to prepare,
    25–6
  choking hazards and, 130
  establishing solid, 6
  finger, 10–2
  forcing, 18
  games with, 24
  having fun with, 22–3
  nutritional guidelines for, 7
  picky eaters of, 27–33
  serving suggestions for, 8–9
  throwing or spitting, 19
  See also Mealtime; Snacks
Freeze dance, 214
Friends
  colds and, 83
  preschool and, 327
  See also Social development
Fruits and vegetables
  establishing solid foods with, 6
  serving suggestions for, 7, 8

G

Games
  animal, 178
  board, 253
  classification, 252
  food, 24
  hide-and-seek, 182
  memory, 246
  sorting, 183
  word, 272
  See also Play
Garbage, 143, 144
Gardening tools, 203
Gender differences, 263, 290–1
Genital play, 116
Gifts
  at birthday parties, 301
  limiting, 173
  for older siblings, 320
Girls vs. boys, 290–1
Grinding food, 6
Gross motor skills
  dance and, 214–5
  dressing and, 234–5
  gender differences and, 290
  playing ball and, 217
  providing opportunities for
    development of, 212–3, 220
  running and jumping, 216
  types of play to develop, 218–9
  walking, 206–9
  See also Fine motor skills
Guns, storing, 135

H

Hammers, 212
Hand washing, 115
Hearing, 273
Heimlich maneuver, 131
HepB vaccine, 76
Hib vaccine, 76
Hide-and-seek, 182
Highchairs, 17
Hitting, 158–9
Hives, fevers and, 81
"Hokey Pokey" song, 215, 235
Home businesses, 334
Home remedies, 84–6
Honesty, 288
Hopping, 218
Hopscotch, 219
Hotels, 364–5
House, playing, 179
Household items
  as choking hazards, 130
  poison awareness and, 128
  used as toys, 187
Humidifiers, 85, 86
Hygiene. *See* Baths; Tooth
  brushing

I

Illnesses
  childcare and, 350–1
  cleanliness and, 83–4
  home remedies for, 84–6
  See also Physical health

Imagination
  dramatic play and, 179–81
  dress-up play and, 190–1
  stimulating, 172–3
Immunizations, 76, 91
Incisors (teeth), 82
Independence
  dressing and, 234–5
  fostering, 295–8
  negativity and, 162
  in the only child, 294
  preschool and, 327
  self-feeding and, 18
Independent thinking, 242
Injuries
  band-aids and, 86
  preventing, 135
  treating minor, 133–4
  See also Safety
Insect stings, 201
Instructions, following, 246
International travel, 366–8
IPV (inactivated polio vaccine), 76
Irritable bowel, 16

J

Juices, limiting, 14
Jumping, 214, 216, 218

K

Kitchen
  child helping in the, 232
  toddler-proofing, 143

L

Language development
  in bilingual families, 264–5
  easing difficulties in, 274–5
  emotional expression and, 311,
    312
  finger play for, 276–9
  hearing issues and, 273
  methods to increase, 264–5,
    268–70, 272
  in the only child, 294
  in twins, 266–7
  See also Vocabulary; Words
Last-born characteristics, 293
Laundry, helping to sort, 232
Leaping, 218
Letters, learning, 282
Limits, setting, 156
Liquid intake
  before bedtime, 62
  early rising and, 68
  fevers and, 81
  overnight dryness and, 121
Lost child, 139
Lotion, 38
Loveys, 58, 63, 87, 352

M

Manners, 19, 325, 326
Massage, 41, 65
Math skills, 250–1
Mealtime
  fostering independence at, 297

P

Pacifier, germs from, 84
Paint(ing)
  bath, 45
  finger, 187, 227
  poster, 227
Parallel play, 169
Parents
  bond with childcare caregiver,
    346–7
  sharing duties, 348–9
  See also Role modeling
Parties, 16, 300–2
PCV (pneumococcal conjugate
    vaccine), 76
Peanut butter, 16
Peanut butter play dough, 230
Pencil grips, 226
Permissive parenting style, 151
Personality, 298–9, 324
Physical health
  fevers and, 80–1
  teething pain and, 82
  temperature taking and, 79–80
  vaccinations and, 76
  See also Doctor; Medication
Pinkeye, home remedy for, 85
Plants, poisonous, 141, 203
Plastic bags, 143
Plates
  gripper, 17
  playful, 23
Play
  with balls, 217

with big boxes, 173, 179
dramatic, 179–81
dressing-up, 190–1
during bath time, 41–3, 45
gender differences and, 291
gross motor, 218–9
imaginative, 172–3
with parents, 192
practicing developmental tasks
    during, 185
puppet, 188–9
sensory-motor, 174–5, 184
stages of, 168–9
See also Games; Outdoor play;
    Toys
Play dates, 170–1
Play dough, 186, 229, 230
Playground, 212
Poison control
  hidden dangers and, 128
  phone number for, 127
  plants and, 141, 203
Popsicles, 81, 83
Positive reinforcement
  at bedtime, 63
  guiding toddler's behavior with,
    163
  language development and, 262
  for not hitting or biting, 159
  See also Praise; Rewards
Poster paints, 227
Potty-chair, 105, 112
Powder, 38
Praise

cognitive skill development
and, 241
during play dates, 171
learning to walk and, 208
for not whining, 161
for overnight dryness, 121
self-esteem and, 284
when showing empathy, 323
See also Positive reinforcement;
Rewards
Prereading skills, 280–2
Preschool, 327–9, 335
Presents. *See* Gifts
Prewriting practice, 230–1
Problem-solving skills, 244–5, 254
Promises, keeping, 289
Protein, 7, 9
Psychological development
birth order and, 292
building trust and, 288–9
nurturing self-esteem, 284–7
in the only child, 294
for the slow to warm up, 298–9
See also Emotions
Pull toys, 186, 194
Puppets, 42, 188–9, 362
Push toys, 186, 194
Puzzles, 186, 233, 250, 254

R

Reading and books
at bedtime, 55, 62
developing prereading skills
and, 280–2

about food, 30
language development and,
267, 268
at level higher than usual, 242
preparing for a doctor visit
with, 87
for toilet training, 109
See also Stories
Rectal thermometer, 79
Relaxation techniques, 55, 72
Relaxation time, 72
Respect, teaching, 156
Restaurants, 34–6
Rewards
bedtime, 55
for staying in bed, 64
for toilet training, 109, 111,
113, 117
See also Positive reinforcement;
Praise
Rhyming, 272
Rituals. *See* Routines
Role modeling
language and, 271, 274
learning new skills and, 245
learning social skills and, 324
at restaurants, 35
Rolling, 213
Routines
bedtime, 54, 59
tooth brushing, 47
Running, 216, 218
Runny nose, home remedy for, 84

S

Safety
  camping and, 363
  childcare providers and, 337
  choking and, 129–31
  discipline and, 155
  first-aid kits and, 132
  lost child and, 139
  medication and, 94–5
  outdoor, 198–9, 202–3
  poison control and, 127, 128
  preventive efforts for, 135–8
  swimming pool, 204
  toys and, 191
  treating minor injuries and,
    133–4
  See also Injuries
Sandbox, 195
Sand play, 174
Scrapes, 133
Scribbling, 226, 230–1
Self-esteem, 284–7
Sensory-motor play, 174, 184
Separation anxiety, 345
Setting the table, 232
Shampooing, 38, 40, 43
Shape box, 187
Shapes
  cutting food into, 11
  drawing simple, 223
  learning, 247
Sharing, 170–1, 325, 327
Shoes
  choosing, 210–1

  tying, 236
  velcro vs. lace, 237
  walking without, 209
Shopping for shoes, 210–1
Sibling rivalry, 320–2
Singing
  in the bathtub, 41, 44
  See also Music
Sizes, learning, 250
Skipping, 214
Sleep
  early rising from, 68–71
  getting back to, 65
  getting toddler to nap, 72–3
  See also Bedtime
Smashed fingers, 133
Smoke detectors, 141
Snacks
  car travel and, 359
  changing eating habits and,
    12–3
  getting back to sleep with, 65
  time of the day for, 13
  See also Food(s)
Social development
  helping to support, 324–6
  play dates and, 170–1
  preschool and, 327–9
  See also Friends
Solid foods. *See* Food(s)
Solitary play, 168
Somersaults, 219
Sore throat, home remedy for, 84
Sorting